Book 1

In the series

Free to be

HOLY

Learning to live in the realm of Truth

Wendy Barwegen

GENESIS REVISITED

Spiritual Truths
uncovered from the creation account
place an entirely different perspective
on the concept of holiness.

Straightforward, logical, and theological answers
to some of Christianity's biggest questions.
Truths exposed so comprehensively
they are impossible to ignore.

Free to be Holy

Copyright 2007 by Wendy Barwegen.
All rights reserved. No portion of this book may be reproduced, stored in a retrieval system, or transmitted in any form or by any means without the express permission of the author except in the case of brief quotations embodied in critical articles and reviews.

ISBN   1-4196-8098-6
ISBN-13   978-1-4196-8098-4

All scripture quotations are taken from the King James Version of the Bible unless otherwise noted.

All Hebrew and Greek definitions are taken from *Strong's Hebrew and Greek Dictionaries* Electronic Edition STEP Files Copyright © 2003, QuickVerse, a division of Findex.com, Inc., all rights reserved.

All English definitions are taken from the Encarta ® World English Dictionary © & (P) 1998-2004 Microsoft Corporation. All rights reserved.

All Charles Spurgeon quotes are taken from his devotional, *All of Grace*.

Scientific details expressed in the seventh chapter are taken from *Basic Science for Christian Schools*, Bob Jones University.

Cover design and technical assistance:
Carol Kaufmann -- Watseka Sign
Chris Meredith -- Techzone, Watseka
Chuck Gomez -- Gomez Productions, Watseka

Cover photography:
Scott Anderson -- AnderSon's Photography, Watseka

THANK YOU

To my Father in Heaven,

I cannot even express to You how honored I am to have sat at Your feet these many years. I love You so.

To my sons,

I have been and continue to be the recipient of your constant encouragement. You are living epistles written on my heart and I adore you.

To my loving husband,

You have been a "very present help" in more ways than I can count. Your steadfast support is deeply appreciated.

To my mentor, Rod Franklin,

You introduced me to a lively faith. I am eternally grateful.

WENDY BARWEGEN

For additional copies visit
www.booksurge.com
or www.amazon.com

For information about other books in this series, or scheduling a speaking engagement, please contact:

Wendy Barwegen

By calling 815.471.2986

wbarwegen@yahoo.com

contents

Preface	ix
Part I: The Logic	1
Introduction	3
1. Is there an echo in here?	7
2. Carnality Calls	45
3. Hell Dust	71
4. Beyond Eden	87
5. A Seed Sown	109
Part II: The Beauty	129
Introduction	131
6. Sin; a necessary evil	137
7. The Passionate Protagonist	165

preface

Do not analyze nor be amazed by the messenger; analyze and be amazed by the Message.

"But God hath chosen
the foolish things of the world
to confound the wise;
and God hath chosen
the weak things of the world
to confound the things which are mighty;
And base things of the world,
and things which are despised,
hath God chosen,
yea, and things which are not,
to bring to nought things that are:
That no flesh should glory in his presence.
But of him are ye in Christ Jesus,
who of God is made unto us wisdom,
and righteousness,
and sanctification, and redemption:
That, according as it is written,
He that glorieth, let him glory in the Lord."

1 Corinthians 1:27 - 31

Dear reader,

What you are about to read is not my opinion. I have scrutinized the subject of holiness for seventeen years. The books contained in the <u>Free to be Holy</u> series come to you as a result of fastidious research, study, and practical application. I am simply passing along my findings and my experiences as I have employed them.

You may agree with my theses or you may not, however, you will be hard pressed to ignore them. Maybe for the first time, God, and the craziness that this life entails, will make sense to you. More importantly, my prayer for you is that your heart will be comforted by the power and majesty of our God.

Please forgive my lack of polish in this manuscript as I am not a professional writer. I hope the contents will make up for the proletarian manner of the text.

God be with you as you pioneer into the mysteries of the Bible.

Sincerely,

Wendy Barwegen

Part I
The Logic

Free to be Holy

Introduction

If one wants to be rid of a weed, one must get it at the root. We see the problem of sin but when we do nothing more than take whacks at what we see, it only grows back bigger and stronger. We fail to see the root of sin because we misunderstand the origins of sin.

In order to understand sin's place in humanity, one must go all the way back to the beginning as it is recorded in Genesis. Genesis is the root of all Truth. All other Biblical Truths build upon this foundational root. As you go through Hell Bent you will be introduced to the God of Adam, and the creation account in a whole new way.

Being the foundation of all Truth, Genesis is an absolute target. And that makes sense. If I am the devil, I am going to try to break the foundation; that way everything else falls as well. Our enemy has done a bang up job. When we get Genesis wrong, everything else has a hard time being right.

Although they have no strong Biblical foundation, the following are commonly taught creation precepts:

- A perfect man, who was formed perfectly by a perfect God went "wrong" simply because he had a choice to go wrong.
- Adam had a bright future full of glory before he sinned. He had endless days of walking together with God in the cool of the day.
- The devil snuck into the Garden of Eden.
- Adam and Eve ate the fruit and everything was ruined.
- God had to figure out a way to salvage the situation.
- If God handled it wrong, He could lose His place of Most High God in eternity. (Yes, I have actually heard that more than once.)
- God salvaged the situation by sending His own Son to die in man's place.
- As we receive forgiveness we are cleansed back to the place where Adam and Eve were before they sinned and we are able to enjoy the same relationship they had with God.
- God cursed the earth, and now under a monumentally worsened set of circumstances, we are left to take Adam and Eve's test every moment of our lives.
- If we are wise, we will learn from their mistake and not eat of

our forbidden fruits.
- When we abstain from our forbidden fruits, the work of Christ brings us back to the Garden of Eden experience.

Scripturally, none of this is accurate. As a matter of fact, none of this is even logical. These common, though mistaken assumptions concerning the events that took place in the first three chapters of Genesis are skewing everything else in the Bible away from Truth.

What I have found is that the good news is so good that it is difficult to believe. The message of the Bible lays the entire burden on God and the entire blessing on us. This is really so hard to accept that we try to come up with alternatives in case we are wrong. When we find an alternative that comes close to the Truth, we practice it as a back up plan hoping that we will at least get points for good intentions. Unfortunately, true faith does not work with a net. We need to embrace the true Gospel and forsake all others.

We are going to look more closely at the events that took place in the first three chapters of Genesis. This will help us understand what really happened in that garden. When we see the Truth, sin will have bared its root.

Free to be Holy

*Thus the heavens and the earth were finished,
and all the host of them.
And on the seventh day God ended his work which he had made;
and he rested on the seventh day
from all his work which he had made.*
Genesis 2:1 - 2

Is there an echo in here?

The entire premise of this book series is found in the understanding of both the spiritual and the natural realms. Everyone acknowledges the fact that there are both spiritual and natural realms, however, our understanding of them is so limited that we are not effectively accessing them.

Beginning in Genesis we are going to study these realms and gain spiritual insights that will draw everything back into line.

Pictures in time

The Old Testament needs to be taken both literally and figuratively. Although it is comprised of stories of actual events, and actual prophecies that have actually taken place, and still other prophecies that will eventually take place, the Old Testament's most prominent purpose is in its masterful images of the spiritual realm and its inerrant Truths.

The single most important thing to understand about these two realms is that in one, everything *is* done and in the other, everything *will be* done. In the spiritual realm all things have been accomplished, whereas in the natural realm, all things have not yet been accomplished. Everything that has ever been done has been done spiritually before it has ever materialized in this natural world. That is just God's way of doing things.

This is not a foreign thought to us. The Bible speaks of many things that are not yet manifested in the natural realm. In each of these, it is always just a matter of time. The Bible says that Jesus took sin out of the world, yet sin is still in the world. Spiritually, sin has been taken out of the world; therefore, we know that there is coming a day when we will see the natural manifestation of this spiritual Truth.

The Bible also says that Jesus bore our griefs and carried our sorrows, yet in this natural realm we still grieve and we still have sorrow. The Bible also says that by His stripes we are healed, yet in this natural realm we still have sickness and disease.

We know that these Biblical precepts are true in the spiritual realm and simply need to be manifested in the natural realm. Jesus chastised His disciples because they could not calm the storm.

Evidently, in the spiritual realm, they had the power to do this, while in the natural they did not. The fact that Jesus chastised them tells us that anyone who is in touch with the spiritual realm can walk in it.

In the very first chapter of the Gospel of John, we have another example of a natural manifestation of a spiritual Truth, and not coincidentally, this chapter begins sounding a lot like Genesis, *"In the beginning was the Word, and the Word was with God, and the Word was God...And the Word was made flesh, and dwelt among us, (and we beheld his glory, the glory as of the only begotten of the Father,) full of grace and truth." (John 1:1&14 KJV)*.

Jesus was existent in the beginning and He was the Word, being with God and being God. Four thousand years after the creation of mankind, He was made flesh and dwelled among men so that those who were alive at that time could behold, or actually see His glory. Jesus existed just as surely before He was born into the natural realm as He did afterward. Jesus, like all else, was existent in the spiritual realm first, then birthed into the natural realm when the timing was right. First spiritual, then natural.

Jesus was crucified in the spiritual realm before He was crucified in the natural, *"And all that dwell upon the earth shall worship him, whose names are not written in the book of life of the Lamb **slain from the foundation of the world**." (Rev 13:8 KJV emphasis mine)*. First spiritual, then natural.

Come again?

Now we must take this information into the creation account found in Genesis. In the first chapter of Genesis, God created all things in six days and then He rested. Right away I have a problem with this. God took only six days to create everything that needed to be created? When we read the Bible, we see a very different usage of time. I don't believe anything has ever happened that fast.

It took twenty-five years for Abraham to receive a promised son. It took forty years for Moses to begin his ministry after he had been called. It took four thousand years for Jesus to be manifested on earth. Four hundreds years passed after Joseph said, *"...God will surely visit you, and ye shall carry up my bones from hence." (Gen 50:25 KJV)*, before those bones were carried.

There were many years between the time that David was anointed to be king and his actual reign over Israel. The flood came one hundred and twenty years after God spoke it to Noah. More than twenty years passed before Joseph's brothers bowed down to him according to his prophetic dream.

I could fill several pages with similar lengthy time spans. It is just not fitting with God's way of doing things to create everything and interact with Adam concerning the animals, the plants, and Eve all in the space of six days!

How is it that God was able to accomplish all of this so quickly? The answer lies in the concept of the spiritual realm. You see, God was creating in the *spiritual* realm on those first six days; not the natural. The spiritual realm has no concept of time; it is in the natural that the concept of time is employed.

This is why we have a somewhat different account of creation in the second chapter of Genesis. You see, in this second chapter we see a repeat of the "creation" of plant life, the fowls of the air, the animal kingdom, and mankind. In this second rendition, things don't happen so quickly.

In preparation for this teaching I read a good number of articles from different commentaries. I found that there were almost as many opinions as there were commentators. In several reports, the fact that the creation account is repeated wasn't even brought into discussion. I know of one main line denomination that believes that the second chapter of Genesis is nothing more than a parable.

It is obvious that many are befuddled by the repeat of creation.

However, the bulk of us believe the second chapter of Genesis is an elaboration of the first chapter. As we are about to see, there are too many differences for this to be true. While it is true that we get more information in the second chapter, I believe the actual formations of plants, animals, fowls, and mankind in this second chapter is a separate occurrence from the original creation account.

As we study the two accounts of creation, we will see that the Scriptures give indication that God created everything firstly in the spiritual realm, and then went on to form particular things in the natural realm when the timing and circumstances were right. First spiritual, then natural.

Jesus was a spiritual God, He was born a natural man, and now He is spiritual again as a Man/God. The apostle Paul tells us, *"...He hath chosen us in him before the foundation of the world..." (Eph 1:4 KJV)*. Therefore, we also existed first in the spiritual realm, we were then born into the natural realm, and finally we get birthed back into the spiritual realm through the born again experience. Everything both has its beginning, and finds its end in the spiritual realm.

The Order of Creation

As the first chapter of Genesis explains the creation account we see that there was a very precise order of creation with particular days assigned to each creation:

Day one: Light
Day two: Atmosphere
Day three: Land, seas, and plant life
Day four: Sun, moon, and stars
Day five: Living creatures to inhabit the skies and seas.
Day six: Beasts of the earth and mankind, both male and female.

At the culmination of these, *"...God saw every thing that he had made, and, behold, it was very good. And the evening and the morning were the sixth day." (Gen 1:31 KJV)*. God saw everything that He had made and assessed that it was "good". We must take note of what the Scriptures make very plain: The order of creation and the fact that God *saw* the creations.

In this creation of mankind, God actually spoke to the man and the woman, *"And God blessed them, and God said unto them, Be fruitful, and multiply, and replenish the earth, and subdue it: and have dominion over the fish of the sea, and over the fowl of the air, and over every living thing that moveth upon the earth." (Gen 1:28 KJV)*. So we see that what happened in the first chapter of Genesis actually happened; God was not speaking to the air. The spiritual realm is a very real place. The spiritual realm, indeed, is more valid than the natural realm.

A little shift

There were no divisions of chapter and verse in the original manuscripts that make up our Holy Bible. The translators of the original writings were the ones who made the divisions. If I were to have divided the Bible into chapters, I would have used the first three verses of Genesis chapter two as the last three verses in chapter one. Many commentators agree with me.

First of all, as you read them you will note that the first three verses of chapter two are more akin to the end of the original creation as it is recorded in chapter one than they are to the beginning of the circumstances in chapter two. After all, the first three verses in chapter two speak solely of how God rested on the seventh day from His creative work that took place in the first six days. These three verses finish out the week.

Secondly, God's name in all of chapter one and in these first three verses of chapter two is *Elohim*, whereas beginning in the fourth verse and through the balance of chapter two, God is referred to as the LORD God or *Jehovah Elohim*. This is a very important distinction.

```
What's in a name?
```

Matthew Henry speaks of this difference in his commentary on the Old Testament, *"All along, in the first chapter, he was called Elohim—a God of power; but now Jehovah Elohim—a God of power and perfection, a finishing God. As we find him known by his name Jehovah when he appeared to perform what he had promised..."*

In the New Scofield Reference Bible it is stated, *"It is significant that the first appearance of the name Jehovah in Scripture follows the creation of man. It was God (Elohim) who said, "Let us make man in our image" (Gen 1:26); but when man, as in Gen 2, is to fill the scene and become dominant over creation, it is the Lord God (Jehovah Elohim) who acts (Gen 2:4ff.). This clearly indicates a special relation of Deity, in His Jehovah character, to man, and all Scripture emphasizes this."*

There are many names for God. Each of these names shows us a different facet of His being. Each name is active in that it offers us a description of Who God is and what He is presently doing. Similarly, a man can be a son, a father, a brother, a friend, an employee, a citizen, and so on.

God Elohim created all things in six days and God Jehovah Elohim proceeded from there. This is another reason why it is significant that the first three verses of the second chapter of Genesis are dealing with the Elohim of the first chapter while the balance of the second chapter deals with Jehovah Elohim.

```
Elohim
```

The name *Elohim* tells us of God's omnipotent place of Most High

God, supreme over all. This is the facet of God Who created everything and put it in order in that first week of creation. I believe that God, Elohim, is the culmination of the Godhead. As the world was being put in order, Father, Son, and Holy Ghost worked as a team, *"Let **us** make man in **our** image, after **our** likeness..."*

We know that God was present at the time of creation, but evidently so was Jesus, *"And to make all men see what is the fellowship of the mystery, which from the beginning of the world hath been hid in God, who **created all things** by Jesus Christ:"* (Eph 3:9 KJV emphasis mine).

In addition to this, Paul, speaking of Jesus, said, *"For **by him were all things created**, that are in heaven, and that are in earth, visible and invisible, whether they be thrones, or dominions, or principalities, or powers: all things were created by him, and for him: And he is before all things, and by him all things consist."* (Col 1:16-17 KJV emphasis mine).

And we know that the Holy Spirit was present from the very first moment, *"And the Spirit of God moved upon the face of the waters"*. From these passages, we conclude that Father, Son, and Holy Ghost were present as *Elohim* during the creation of the heavens and the earth and all the host of them.

The name Elohim is a plural of the Hebrew "'eloahh", which means deity or God. In other words, *Elohim* is "Gods".

Jehovah Elohim

The name *Jehovah* brings with it many descriptions of God. As a matter of fact, I don't know of a more intricate name for God than *Jehovah*. In Adam Clarke's Commentary on the Old Testament we read, *"Wherever this word occurs in the sacred writings we translate it Lord, which word is, through respect and reverence, always printed in capitals. Though our English term Lord does not give the particular meaning of the original word, yet it conveys a strong and noble sense. Lord is a contraction of the Anglo-Saxon, Hlaford, afterwards written Loverd, and lastly Lord, from bread; hence our word loaf, and ford, to supply, to give out. The word, therefore, implies the giver of bread, i.e., he who deals out all the necessaries of life."* One cannot deal out something that does not already exist.

According to Adam Clarke's commentary, there are eleven attributes contained in the name *Jehovah*. I found these attributes to be sobering and encouraging all at the same time:

1. The strong or mighty God.
2. The merciful Being who is full of tenderness and compassion.
3. The gracious One; he whose nature is goodness itself; the loving God.
4. Long-suffering; the Being who, because of his goodness and tenderness, is not easily irritated, but suffers long and is kind.
5. The great or mighty One.
6. The bountiful Being; he who is exuberant in his beneficence.
7. The truth or true One; he alone who can neither deceive nor be deceived, who is the fountain of truth, and from whom all wisdom and knowledge must be derived.
8. The preserver of bountifulness; he whose beneficence never ends, keeping mercy for thousands of generations, showing compassion and mercy while the world endures.
9. He who bears away iniquity and transgression and sin: properly, the Redeemer, the Pardoner, the Forgiver; the Being whose prerogative alone it is to forgive sin and save the soul.
10. The righteous Judge, who distributes justice with an impartial hand, with whom no innocent person can ever be

Free to be Holy

condemned.
11. He who visits iniquity, who punishes transgressors, and from whose justice no sinner can escape. The God of retributive and vindictive justice.

So we see that the addition of the name *Jehovah* to the name *Elohim* is a significant one. Although Elohim is the Supreme creative Godhead, it is Jehovah Elohim who is tremendously active with mankind. Elohim created the heavens and the earth and all the host of them in the first chapter of Genesis, and then Jehovah Elohim brought these creations into the natural realm when He saw fit to meet the needs of His chosen people. This process will be continued until such a time as the spiritual realm entirely overcomes the natural realm. In that day, death will be swallowed up in victory.

Listen up!

Hence, the following verses are the final commentary on the original creation account, *"Thus the heavens and the earth were finished, and all the host of them. And on the seventh day God ended his work which he had made; and he rested on the seventh day from all his work which he had made. And God blessed the seventh day, and sanctified it: because that in it he had rested from all his work which God created and made." (Gen 2:1-3 KJV).*

In this brief sequence of verses, we notice a great deal of emphasis being placed on the fact that everything was finished and God rested. Three times we are reminded of the completion, *"Thus the **heavens and the earth were finished, God ended his work** which he had made, and God...rested from all **his work which God created and made**..."* and twice we are reminded of God's rest from His work, *"God ended his work...and **he rested on the seventh day**, And God blessed the seventh day, and sanctified it: because that in it **he had rested from all his work** which God created and made."*

When we read the Bible, we must read it like any other letter. If I get a letter from a friend and this friend repeats something several times in short sequence, I am apt to think that she is making a point that she wants very much for me to get.

In these final remarks about the creation in the spiritual realm, it is clear that God wanted us to get the fact that what He had done was finished to the point that He could rest from *all* his work. Creation was finished in six days. Period. The fourth verse of chapter two begins an entirely different account.

The segue

Due to the fact that the first three verses of chapter two are actually the closing remarks of chapter one, the fourth verse is now our opening statement concerning the second creation account. This segue verse teaches us exactly how these two creation accounts interact with one another.

We are going to do some serious word study with this very important verse. We could look to see what someone else might say, but if we go straight to the original language we eliminate the middleman and the propensity for error. The Strong's Concordance, which we will use ad nauseam, is an excellent aid for this purpose.

The following is our segue from Elohim's rest from His creation in the spiritual realm to Jehovah Elohim's birthing of the same in the natural realm according to Genesis 2:4:

> *"These are the generations of the heavens and of the earth when they were created, in the day that the LORD God made the earth and the heavens,"*

The King James wording seems to translate into "The following is how it went when God created everything." From this we make the assumption that what we are about to read is how it went when God created everything. However, there are a few problems with this interpretation.

The word "generations" in Hebrew is taken from the root word "yalad" which means, *to bear young; causatively to beget; medically to act as midwife.* That is why the Hebrew word for "generations" is "tol^{e}dah tol^{e}dah" which, among other things, means "birth". So now instead of *"These are the **generations** of the heavens and the earth...",* we have, *"These are the **birthings** of the heavens and the earth..." (paraphrase).*

Additionally, the word "made" is the Hebrew word, "aśah" which means, *to bring forth.* So now instead of *"Jehovah Elohim **made** the earth and the heavens..."* we have *"Jehovah Elohim **brought forth** the earth and the heavens."*

When we put these two Hebrew definitions together we come up with something like this, *"This is the birth process of the creations of the heavens and the earth in the day that Jehovah Elohim acted as a midwife and brought forth the earth and the heavens."* In this one verse we have gone from Elohim to Jehovah Elohim and from "created" to "made".

Now our verse sounds more like Elohim *created* all things in the spiritual realm in the first week of creation and then Jehovah Elohim entered the scene and *acted as a midwife* and birthed these creations into the natural realm.

One cannot bring forth and act as a midwife unless conception has taken place. Something must exist before it can be brought forth and something must exist before a midwife is needed. One cannot bring forth a thing unless there is a "thing" to bring forth. As well, one does not call a midwife until conception has taken place and a baby is ready to be born. An unborn baby is no less a creation of God than a born baby. We understand this in the natural. God uses the natural things of this world to educate us concerning spiritual things.

The creations of Elohim existed as surely as they would ever exist in the spiritual realm. Now it is time for Jehovah Elohim to bring them forth into the natural realm when the time is right for their "birth". Genesis chapter one told us of the creative works of Elohim in the spiritual realm and now Genesis chapter two tells us of the birthing works of Jehovah Elohim into the natural realm. First spiritual, then natural.

Out of order

Within this segue verse we have another peculiarity, *"These are the generations of the **heavens and of the earth** when they were created, in the day that the LORD God made the **earth and the heavens...**"* Why did we go from "heavens and earth" to" earth and heavens"?

When one runs into a change of order in the exact same verse where the description of the deity and the verb is also changed, one must pay attention to this change. At the very least we must acknowledge that this scripture is giving us ample indication that the creation account that follows is not one and the same as the original. No, something different is about to happen with all the same stuff.

I believe there is even more to this change in order. In his first book to the Corinthians, Paul says, *"As is the earthy, such are they also that are earthy: and as is the heavenly, such are they also that are heavenly." (1 Cor 15:48 KJV).* This verse suggests that the word "earthy" denotes the natural and the word "heavenly" denotes the spiritual. With this in mind I am tempted to think that the other reason we have a change in the order of "heavens and earth" is because we are about move into the next progression of creation.

Now we must see if this makes sense. Elohim created the *spiritual* so that Jehovah Elohim could bring forth the birth of the same in the *natural*; heavens and then earth. Then Jehovah Elohim formed the *natural* so that the Holy Ghost could birth the same into the *spiritual*; earth and then heavens.

Mankind was created spiritually by Elohim, then formed naturally by Jehovah Elohim, then re-created back into the spiritual realm by the Holy Ghost, *"For we are his workmanship, created in Christ Jesus..." (Eph 2:10 KJV)*. It looks like we have been the workmanship of the entire Trinity. Why not?

Father, Son, and Holy Ghost

I can't help but to notice the sequence of the Godhead. We commonly prescribe the following order to the Trinity: Father, Son, and Holy Ghost. Do we see the work of the Father in creation, Jesus in formation, and the Holy Ghost finalizing the whole process through the re-birth in the New Testament?

It would make sense. God is Spirit and He created us in the spiritual realm. Jesus was a natural Man and He formed us in the natural. The Holy Spirit is a Spirit and He births us back into the spiritual realm through the born-again experience.

Father

It is natural to think of Elohim, the Creator of the heavens and the earth, as God the Father. Elohim rested from *all His work* on the seventh day. We cannot make the assumption that this Member of the Trinity at any time broke His rest. Therein is the beauty of the Trinity. While God the Son provides the way and God the Spirit fully enters our wilderness to be with us, God the Father, being fully in control, is at the same time sitting upon His throne resting in all He has done because He knows He has done enough.

God the Father is resting and everything is working together to bring us to a place where we can rest as He is resting, *"For we which have believed do enter into rest, as he said, As I have sworn in my wrath, if they shall enter into my rest: although the works were finished from the foundation of the world."* *(Heb 4:3 KJV)*. The works were finished from the foundation of the world in creation and now Elohim is resting. His will is that we would enter this particular sabbatical. Elohim is the Creator, *"Our Father Who art in Heaven."*

Holy Ghost

We know that the Holy Spirit is with us presently in this dispensation of time. Jesus clearly stated that He was going to leave so that the Father could send the Comforter, that is, the Holy Spirit to indwell and empower mankind.

The Holy Spirit was sent to remind us of everything that Jesus had said, *"These things have I spoken unto you, being yet present with you. But the Comforter, which is the Holy Ghost, whom the Father will send in my name, he shall teach you all things, and bring all things to your remembrance, whatsoever I have said unto you."* *(John 14:25-26 KJV)*.

It is with the Holy Spirit that the Christian has communion or fellowship. According to the Scriptures, we who are born again are born of the Spirit. The Father began everything through creation and the Holy Spirit brings it to an end through re-creating us in Christ.

Son

So now we have both ends of the Book: Father; Creator and Holy Spirit; Indweller. And Who is the Book about? Jesus. From beginning to end the Bible is a Book about Jesus. The life, death, resurrection, and ascension of Jesus is chronicled in the Bible from His eternal existence to that moment in time when every knee will bow, *"I am Alpha and Omega, the beginning and the end, the first and the last." (Rev 22:13 KJV).*

The entire Old Covenant was symbolic of the work of Christ. Everything in the Ark of the Covenant and in the Temple was symbolic of His life, death, and resurrection. We actually see Jesus in person in the book of Daniel, *"He answered and said, Lo, I see four men loose, walking in the midst of the fire, and they have no hurt; and the form of **the fourth is like the Son of God**." (Dan 3:25 KJV emphasis mine).* Finally, we refer back to our definition of "Jehovah" and we find these words, *"he who bears away iniquity and transgression."*

Every story, every Psalm, every prophecy, and every Book speaks of the Messiah and how everything is hinging on Him. Jesus is the meat in the God sandwich. Everything pointed to Jesus in the Old Testament. The New Testament is named the "Gospel" because it speaks the good news concerning Jesus. All of the Old and all of the New point to Jesus.

Jesus was the active Force beginning in the formation of man and continuing throughout the Old Testament until that moment when He left the earth, sent the Holy Ghost, and joined His Father in Heaven. Father, Son, and Holy Ghost….in that order.

When Jesus was conceived by the Holy Ghost and birthed into the earth, He was essentially birthed from the spiritual realm into the natural realm.

Taking turns

God the Father created all things together with Jesus and the Holy Spirit. God, being finished with His work, went to Heaven and sat down on His throne. Jesus stayed behind with the aid of the Holy Spirit to empower the whole operation and bring into manifestation the things of the spiritual realm.

HELL BENT

In this last dispensation, Jesus joins His Father and sits at His right hand waiting till his enemies be made His footstool. Jesus has joined His Father's rest. Before He left, He promised to send the Holy Spirit, which He did. The Father provided all things, the Son opened the way, and the Spirit works with us to continue the task of bringing the blessings of the spiritual realm into the natural.

Now, through the death and resurrection of Christ, we are invited to boldly unite with the Holy Spirit and join the Father and the Son in the throne room, *"Let us therefore come boldly unto the throne of grace, that we may obtain mercy, and find grace to help in time of need." (Heb 4:16 KJV)*.

What we have learned from our segue verse is that God the Father created all things, rested on His throne, and then passed the baton to Jehovah Elohim. It is now time to watch this God birth these creations into the natural realm.

The second creation account

You will notice that the time arrangement in the second creation account is very different than that of the first. The sequence of this second account is out of order. Although the first chapter of Genesis is very particular about assigning days to each creation, the second chapter seems to go out of its way to skew this order. This is one more indication that these creation accounts are different.

Problems already?

Immediately following our segue verse we are met with a peculiar situation, *"And every plant of the field before it was in the earth, and every herb of the field before it grew: for the LORD God had not caused it to rain upon the earth, and there was not a man to till the ground." (Gen 2:4-5 KJV)*. What? No plants?

We know that God, Elohim, created the plant life and *saw* it on the third day of creation, *"And God said, Let the earth bring forth grass, the herb yielding seed, and the fruit tree yielding fruit after his kind, whose seed is in itself, upon the earth: and it was so.* ***And the earth brought forth grass, and herb yielding seed after his kind, and the tree yielding fruit, whose seed was in itself, after his kind: and God <u>saw</u> that it was good."*** *(Gen 1:11-12 KJV).*

God had already created the plant life and saw that it was good and yet we have barren ground right off the bat in this second chapter. So here we have what appears to be a contradiction. In this one verse we went from full-grown herbs and trees with seeds within them to no herbs and no trees.

Because we now understand the functions of the spiritual and the natural realms, we realize that God Elohim spoke everything into being in that first week of creation and as He spoke, those creations became real in the spiritual realm where all Truth begins. The absence of the plant life in this second chapter should be of no concern.

Visible and Invisible

This does not necessarily mean that these creations were apparent in the natural realm. God created all things, *"...**that are in heaven, and that are in earth, visible and invisible**..." (Col 1:16 KJV emphasis mine).* Heavenly things are visible to God even while their earthly counterparts may be invisible.

Just because we cannot yet see a thing does not mean that it has not been created or that it is not visible in the spiritual realm. This is exactly why the apostle Paul tells us, *"While we look not at the things which are seen, but at the things which are not seen: for the things which are seen are temporal; but the things which are not seen are eternal." (2 Cor 4:18 KJV).* The things of the spiritual realm that we do not see are eternal, absolutely apparent, and very real to God.

This is true of all prophecy. The entire book of Revelation is a prophetic story of events that have already taken place in the spiritual realm. John spoke to us concerning things that he *saw*, not things he was *told*. The happenings in Revelation have already taken place in the spiritual realm.

This is why prophecy is dead on accurate. Prophecy speaks of things that already exist in the spiritual realm. We must understand the finality of it. The spiritual realm **will** manifest in the natural realm; there is no question about it.

God always speaks a thing into reality first, and then Jehovah Elohim brings it to pass in the natural realm when the timing and circumstances are ready for it. It is not good when a baby is birthed before he is ready to be birthed. There are no premature births in God's kingdom.

So what we are left with is a sort of spiritual storehouse which Elohim filled with His creations in the first chapter of Genesis and then, in this second chapter, a manifestation, or a birthing, of those things by Jehovah Elohim. First spiritual, then natural. It just makes good sense that God would initiate His story about mankind by stocking the spiritual realm with all that he would need. Jehovah Jireh, our Provider is a very capable Father.

Timing is everything

And so, although God had already created the plant life and saw that it was good and even went so far as to show it to Adam and Eve and speak with them about it, we see that in this second chapter, this plant life was not yet apparent in the natural realm. You see, the timing wasn't right, *"for the LORD God had not caused it to rain upon the earth, and there was not a man to till the ground."*

God purposed that natural weather and natural man would sustain plant life in the natural realm. It is for this reason that what was true in the spiritual realm was not yet apparent in the natural; this baby was still in the Father's womb. Two other "babies" needed to be birthed before the plant life could be brought forth: Water and man.

If we were to look at a barren field we would tend to think that we had a problem. God, Jehovah Elohim, looked at this barren ground and began His role as a mid-wife. Jehovah Elohim pulled from His storehouse in the spiritual realm to solve His "problem", *"...there went up a mist from the earth, and watered the whole face of the ground. And the LORD God formed man of the dust of the ground, and breathed into his nostrils the breath of life; and man became a living soul." (Gen 2:6-7 KJV).*

The ground was barren because plant life needed moisture and a man in the natural realm. Jehovah Elohim was able to provide these things because He knew where to get them.

Because Elohim had already spoken these things into existence in the six days of creation, Jehovah Elohim, the *"Provider of the necessaries of life"*, was now able to act as the midwife and birth them into the natural the moment they were needed, *"...A mist went up and the Lord God formed man..."*

Adam's first breath

Notice that created man now became a living soul or a living and breathing creature, *"...and man **became** a living soul."* Isn't it interesting that Jehovah Elohim breathed into Adam's nostrils the breath of life? This incidence did not take place in the original creation account. The moment natural babies are birthed, they breathe for the very first time. Not so with spiritual babies.

The instant Adam was birthed into the natural realm by Jehovah Elohim the Midwife, He breathed into Adam's nostrils the breath of life and Adam breathed for the first time. Up until this moment, Adam was still in the womb of Elohim -- very much created, but not yet birthed.

The creation and construction of mankind: Speaking vs. forming

In the first instance of Adam's creation, we read how God "created" mankind, *"...So God created man in his own image, in the image of God created he him; male and female created he them."* Elohim spoke and then created. Words became creative entities that existed whole and complete in the spiritual realm.

The Hebrew word for "created" simply means what it has been translated to mean: Created. According to the Encarta World Dictionary, the primary definition of the word "create" is "to bring somebody or something into existence." Elohim did exactly that; He made something that had never before existed. Mankind was a new creation.

Only One Creator

The creation of the Atom Bomb existed solely in the minds of the creators until such a time as they gave it a physical form. Even before it was actually built, it was a reality in the minds of those who created it. The Atom Bomb existed in that it was created; it simply needed a form.

Others have *formed* the Atom Bomb since the United States created it, however, none of these can make the claim that they *created* the Atom Bomb. Others can make, fashion, build, and put together an atom bomb but they cannot create what has already been created. Mankind was *created* perfect in the spiritual realm and then *formed* in the natural.

When it was time to form the first man, Jehovah Elohim did not create a man because man was already created. Instead, Jehovah

Elohim pulled from Elohim's storehouse in the spiritual realm and *formed* the first man in the natural realm.

What we must also note is the fact that the first creation account did not mention being formed of the dust of the earth, nor did it mention any laws, nor did it make reference to any trees in particular. Very generically, man was made, *male and female created He them* and then He gave them supremacy over the earth.

We see that in the first chapter of Genesis, Elohim *created* man, blessed him, gave him supremacy over all other living creatures, and then God saw what He had made and deemed it very good. All of mankind was made "good" on that sixth day of creation. In the spiritual realm we were made perfectly. Now in the second instance of Adam's "creation", we read how Jehovah Elohim *formed* a man. So we had a perfect *creation* and now we have a *formation* of this perfection.

Speaking vs. growing

Now that Jehovah Elohim has taken care of the gardening situation by apprehending the necessary creations in the spiritual realm, *"...the LORD God planted a garden eastward in Eden; and there he put the man whom he had formed. And out of the ground made the LORD God to grow every tree that is pleasant to the sight, and good for food; the tree of life also in the midst of the garden, and the tree of knowledge of good and evil." (Gen 2:8-9 KJV)*.

In the first chapter of Genesis, God (Elohim) *spoke* concerning the creation of the plant life. Elohim said, in the original language, *"Earth, bring forth grass, herbs, and fruit trees...and the earth brought forth grass, herbs, and fruit trees yielding fruit of its kind whose seed is in itself."* (paraphrase). So we see that Elohim spoke, and at that moment plants already containing seeds were created. God's spoken Word is the beginning of everything.

Now in this second chapter we see that Jehovah Elohim did not speak, rather He *planted* a garden in which He *put* the man whom He had *formed* and then, *out of the ground made the LORD God to grow...* Elohim's job was to speak creation into reality in the spiritual realm and Jehovah Elohim's job was to act as the Midwife and bring forth this reality into the natural realm through the processes of *planting, putting, forming, making, and growing*; in other words, *naturally.*

Because Elohim had created all the mature plant life with seeds of like kind within each one, Jehovah Elohim was able to take these seeds from the spiritual realm to plant this garden in Eden, *"...the LORD God planted a garden eastward in Eden."*

The spiritual realm is a perfect realm, never in a state of transition. Once Elohim decrees a thing, it becomes true in the most absolute sense. When that thing is manifested, it is no more true or real than it was before it was manifested. Although we know that the timing of the birth, death, resurrection, ascension, and return of Christ in this natural realm has been and will be extremely precise, in the spiritual realm, not only have these things already taken place, but they took place before we took place!

Another problem?

Now that Adam was formed and tending a flourishing garden, we come to a curious place where Jehovah Elohim sees another need, *"And the LORD God said, It is not good that the man should be alone..."* In order to meet this need, Jehovah Elohim says, *"I will make him an help meet for him."* and then He proceeds, *"And out of the ground the LORD God formed every beast of the field, and every fowl of the air..." (Gen 2:18-19a KJV).*

Again, this is a true contradiction if we do not keep in mind the parallel realities. Jehovah Elohim looked at man, deemed him in need of a partner, and then proceeded to *form* the beasts of the field and the fowl of the air.

However, in the original account of creation, the beasts and fowl were created *before* Adam was created. On the fourth day, *"...God said...let the....fowl...fly above the earth in the open firmament of heaven... And God created...every winged fowl after his kind..."* And on the sixth day, before Adam was created, *"...**God made the beast** of the earth after his kind, and cattle after their kind, and **every thing that creepeth upon the earth** after his kind."* So here we have another instance where things that were already created in the spiritual realm had not yet been birthed into the natural.

After Jehovah Elohim brought forth the beasts of the field and the birds of the air by birthing them into the natural realm, He brought them to Adam one by one for Adam to name them, *"...and whatsoever Adam called every living creature, that was the name thereof. And Adam gave names to all cattle, and to the fowl of the air, and to every beast of the field..."* (Gen 19b-20a KJV).

Help, yes; *helpmeet*? No.

Our omniscient God knew that none of these would be sufficient as a help meet. However, the animal kingdom is the one part of creation that is the most akin to mankind. Earth, sky, plants, sun, moon, stars, seas and the inhabitants thereof...these are all very different from mankind. However, the beasts of the field and the fowl of the air all breathe our air, and have eyes, ears, noses, mouths, thinking brains, and feeling hearts.

We must consider the fact that Adam was a brand new creation. He did not know the rules; therefore, he needed to be taught the rules. God wanted to make it very clear to Adam that these creations had a particular purpose and that purpose was not to be his helpmeet.

The Scripture is very plain in saying that the living creatures were brought before Adam for the purpose of seeing what Adam would call each one and then naming them likewise. In other words, God introduced Adam to each creation individually and showed Adam their purpose in the earth. It was from this information that Adam named each one of them and understood his non-helpmeet relationship with them.

Probably the best example of this naming process is found in the naming of the Anteater. Jehovah Elohim showed Adam this creature that was going about eating ants and Adam said, "Anteater"! Many animals' names are derived from a characteristic. In showing Adam the purpose of each animal and each fowl, Jehovah Elohim also showed Adam that none of these were to be his helpmeet.

Ready, set, go!

If these animals were formed before the formation of Eve, as we see here that they have been, then we must consider a serious time situation in the original account of creation. The sixth day of the original creation began with Elohim creating the all the beasts of the field and the man. Are we to suppose that in the balance of that one day, Adam had time to learn and name all these beasts and the all the fowl, with time left over to have a woman surgically removed from his side? This is not likely.

I have recently watched a special on television called *Planet Earth*. In this very well made series, one cannot help but to take lessons from God and be awed by His handiwork. As well, I have heard numerous Biblical teachings about many animals and birds and how their instinctive behaviors positively scream of the ways, presence, and glory of God.

The Bible itself uses animals and birds to teach Biblical concepts. I cannot even imagine what it was like for Adam to have this up close and personal seminar presented to him from the very mouth of Jehovah Elohim.

I am confident that God did not move through this scene at the speed of light. I am sure that Jehovah Elohim and Adam took their time as they studied each beast and every fowl together. This was before Adam sinned. There were no wife and kids; it was just God and His man. Time was not an issue. Considering the vast numbers of species and the intricacies of each, I honestly cannot imagine that anything less than years were devoted to this monumental task. W must remember the nature of God.

No helpmeet

At the culmination of this task, Adam's emotional needs were not addressed, *"...but for Adam there was not found an help meet for him." (Gen 2:20 KJV)*. The animal kingdom can be a "help" to Adam, however it cannot be a "help meet". According to the Hebrew definition, another word for *helpmeet* is "counterpart". Adam needed a counterpart, which means God thought it good that Adam be *connected* somehow to another being.

Male and Female

The first human was made in the image of God. What this tells us is that this human was just like God. If God thought it good that this human not be alone, we must take this as a commentary about God. God thought it good that *He* not be alone, but rather that *He* would be in relationship with someone who could be *His* help meet, or *His* counterpart.

God proved this by making a human in His image and then putting Himself in a relationship with that human. God thought it good that *He* not be alone. When He made man, God saw him and said that he was "good". *"Not good to be alone"*....create man -- *"and God saw that it was good"*.

In the same way that God brought forth us from Him, He brought forth Eve from Adam. This is why we are being absorbed back into God through marriage in the New Testament. Eve was to be Adam's counterpart and we are to be God's counterpart. It is for this reason that we are called the bride of Christ.

We are counterparts to God in the same way that Eve was counterpart to Adam. What Adam and Eve experienced was nothing more than a natural example demonstrating a spiritual truth.

Woman

With the formation of woman, a human was split into two parts. The word "man", as it is used in the first chapter of Genesis, simply means a human being, not of a particular gender. When God spoke of creating "man", He used the word "adam" (human). When God spoke of making male and female He used the words "zakar" (male) and "n^{e}qebah" (female). If we replace the English words with the words in Hebrew they would read like this, *"So God created human beings, male and female created He them."*

Therefore, when Jehovah Elohim needed a helpmeet for Adam, He went to His heavenly storehouse where male and female were already created. I believe that Jehovah Elohim explained to Adam what He was going to do and then, *"...the LORD God caused a deep sleep to fall upon Adam, and he slept: and he took one of his ribs, and closed up the flesh instead thereof; And the rib, which the LORD God had taken from man, made he a woman, and brought her unto the man." (Gen 2:21-22 KJV).*

We know that the human, "adam", was called adam simply because that is the Hebrew word for human, however, Moses, the penman of Genesis, *named* the first human "Adam" in this key verse. Prior to this verse, the word "adam" was defined as, *ruddy, that is, a human being.* However, in this verse the same word which is translated "Adam" has this Hebrew definition: *Adam, the name of the first man.* A baby is named only after he is born.

The next thing we must notice is the word "made" where it concerned Eve. That word in Hebrew is "banah" and means, *to build or to obtain children.* In the first chapter Elohim *created* the male and the female, and now in this second chapter Jehovah Elohim *molded* (yatsar) man and *built to obtain children* (banah) female. First came the creation in the spiritual realm, next came the molding and the building in the natural realm.

Split to multiply

I said earlier that God told Adam what He was going to do with him before He took Eve from his side. The proof of this is in what Adam said the moment Jehovah Elohim brought this female to Adam, "*...Adam said, This is now bone of my bones, and flesh of my flesh: she shall be called Woman, because she was taken out of Man. Therefore shall a man leave his father and his mother, and shall cleave unto his wife: and they shall be one flesh."* (Gen 2:23-24 KJV). Adam knew exactly from whence Eve came the instant he saw her. Adam knew that he had been split in two.

Let me use the Hebrew definitions to rephrase what Adam said when he saw Eve, "Adam said, this is now bone of my bones, and flesh of my flesh. She shall be called female and be a wife because she was taken out of a male. Therefore shall a male (iysh) leave his father and mother and shall cleave unto his female ('ishsha^hnashıym) wife and they shall be one flesh." Up until this point, this particular word for male, "iysh" had not been used. There was an adam, then there was a surgery, then there was an iysh and an 'ishsha^hnashıym. Or, in layman's terms, there was a human, then there was a surgery, then there was male and female.

Neither male nor female

I say all of that to say this: If God made a human in His image and then split that human into male and female parts, we must draw the conclusion that God is neither male nor female. If God were a male, He would not have been able to create His human is such a way that an entire female entity could be taken out of him. God is neither male nor female. God is. That is all. God is.

In the book of Numbers, Moses says, *"God is not a man, that he should lie; neither the son of man, that he should repent..."* In the first instance, we have the male version of man, iysh, and in the second, the human version of man, adam.

In other words, this verse reads like this, *"God is not a male that He should lie, neither the son of a human that He should repent..."* God is a God. He is not a male, nor is He even a human and He makes this clear in this verse. Jesus was a man when He was born into the earth, but that is because He was a blend between man and God.

God pulled from Himself and formed a human in His image and then He split that human in two and made one half male and the other half female. God has assumed the male role and given us the female role because He took us out of Him in the same way that He took Eve out of Adam. Every spiritual thing has a natural counterpart. The natural exists to give form to the spiritual.

The marriage relationship, like everything else, teaches us about God's eternal power and Godhead. The two, Adam and Eve, became one flesh and the two, God and man became one, *"That they all may be one; as thou, Father, art in me, and I in thee, that they also may be one in us" (John 17).*

God went on to use the concept of exponential growth to expand humanity, and Himself, eternally. God split Himself so that there were two. Then God split the man and there were three. Then Adam and Eve came together and the exponential growth began to fill the earth with the bride of Christ; the counterpart to the Most

High God.

No male chauvinist

God likens Himself to the male side of creation simply because the entire point of creating man was to have a relationship and a relationship requires that roles be played. There are parent and child, brother and sister, husband and wife, and friends. Anywhere that there is fondness there must also be relationship. This is why God is our Father, our Brother, our Husband, and our Friend.

Biblically, the father is the provider, the brother is the protector, the husband is the lover, and a friend will lead (see Proverbs). God took a male role in our relationship because He wanted to provide, protect, love, and lead His dear creation.

This does not mean that God is a male; it simply means that He has assumed that role in much the same way that He assumed the role of a lamb. Although God is not a lamb, He took and lived that role to show us the level of sacrifice to which He would submit Himself. God has assumed the male role to help us relate to and understand Him properly. God is not a man; God is God.

What's my motivation?

Biblically the male has the dominant role. This is not to say that males are more important than females. The male named "Adam" was only half a person when Eve was taken from him. Females are equally as important as males. However, God always has everything in order; not an order of importance mind you....just an order. The letter "A" is no more important than the letter "B" although the letter "A" comes before the letter "B" in the alphabet.

Now it is true that God is more important than us. That sentence does not even justify the concept. He is, has always been, and ever will be Most High God.

However, men are not more important than women, parents are not more important than children, older siblings are not more important than the younger and your friend is not more important than you. We have simply each been given roles to play at different times of our lives for the purpose of demonstrating to us how to relate to God properly.

As children we learn how to relate to God as our Father. As siblings we learn how to relate to Jesus as our Brother. As friends we learn how to relate to the Holy Spirit. Through marriage we learn how to relate to God our Husband.

`Not so bad after all`

To the world it appears as though wives, children, and younger siblings have the short end of the stick in that they are to be subservient to husbands, fathers, and older siblings. However, these actually have an ideal opportunity to gain knowledge from these roles to empower them to access God as their Husband, Father, and big Brother.

This is why, typically, women have an easier time relating to God as a husband. Women have practiced the role of being a wife in life. As well, the younger a person is, the more apt he is to respond to God as a child. A child is familiar with playing the role of a child. The adult man has not practiced being a wife and child; he is out of his element!

However, what men lack by not being wives and a children they make up for in being providers and leaders. In this way they get to experience playing the role of "God". Men understand the burden of provision and protection. Men deal with disobedience and the ensuing discipline. Men have to lead these who have been left in their charge. Men have a much better idea of what it is like to be God than do women.

So we see that in our roles with God, we learn about Him in ways that we can, and should teach each other. In this very important way we need each other. Imagine a world where men teach their wives and children how God relates to them, and women and children teach men how to relate to God. We are counterparts.

Men, women, and children simply have roles to play as examples of what is really taking place in the spiritual realm. These roles need never be issues or bondages when we understand them. In the spiritual realm, *"There is neither Jew nor Greek, there is neither bond nor free, there is neither male nor female: for ye are all one in Christ Jesus." (Gal 3:28 KJV)*.

Jesus knew how to walk this line. He was well aware that His role was that of a Son Who is subservient to His Father. Jesus attributed all authority to God and did not exalt Himself above Him, *"...I do nothing of myself; but as my Father hath taught me, I speak these things." (John 8:28b KJV)*. At the same time Jesus worked the works of God because He, *"...thought it not robbery to be equal with God." (Phil 2:5)*.

The God Who owns all authority wants to give that very authority to mankind. God is not trying to hold back through authorities; it is through our relationship with them that God is showing us how to access all that He is!

So we see that from the very beginning of creation God has been teaching us how His kingdom works by creating all things in the spiritual realm and manifesting these very things in the natural realm. The reason everything on earth speaks of God is because everything on earth issued from Him and His realm of spiritual Truth.

Timing

As we studied this second account of "creation" we noticed that the order was purposefully rearranged. In the initial account, plant life was created, followed by the fowl of the air, the beasts of the field, then the creation of mankind, both male and female in that order.

However, in the account we just read, man was first formed, then the garden brought forth life, then the beasts of the field and fowl of the air were formed, then Eve was formed. We went from *plants-fowl-beasts-man-woman* to *man-plants-beasts-fowl-woman*. This order is very different.

Just because the things of the spiritual realm were created in a particular order does not mean their manifestations in the natural realm have to be in that order. When we read the Prophets, we notice that many things were spoken in a much different sequence than they were later manifested. Short term prophecies and long term prophecies run side by side throughout the Bible. This mix up in order need not be a problem for those who consider the spiritual realm.

Time has been given to the natural realm and that is why time is employed in the natural realm. The spiritual realm knows no time and therefore does not bind itself to time. We remember that the things that exist in the spiritual realm are eternal whereas the things that exist in the natural realm are temporary and are ruled by seconds, minutes, hours, days, weeks, months, years, decades, centuries, and millennia.

Lessons everywhere

The first chapter of Romans tells us that, *"For the invisible things of him from the creation of the world are clearly seen, being understood by the things that are made..."* Everything around us speaks of the invisible things of God from the creation of the world. We understand the Truths of the spiritual realm by studying the things that are "made" in the natural realm.

Whether we are dealing with relationships, geology, the human body, the animal, fish, or bird kingdom, the weather, our natural environment, or science of any kind, we run into spiritual parallels.

What this tells me is that, not just some things, but *everything* in this natural realm exists to teach us a lesson about the spiritual realm. I believe this is what the creation account is demonstrating.

The entire Old Testament is a pictoral guide for the born-again Christian. All one has to do to see how God responds to His children is look to see how He responded to Israel because the nation of Israel was the Old Testament type of the New Testament Christian. The Old Testament wilderness was a type of our wilderness time when we aren't sure where we are going. The Old Testament Promised Land was a type of our promised land where all spiritual blessings are waiting for us in heavenly places!

Moses was admonished to fashion the Tabernacle after the real Tabernacle in heaven; God had a pattern of it, *"Who serve unto the example and shadow of heavenly things, as Moses was admonished of God when he was about to make the tabernacle: for, See, saith he, that thou make all things according to the pattern showed to thee in the mount." (Heb 8:5 KJV)*. As well, the Mosaic Law and the Levitical priesthood were only a shadow of good things to come through the resurrection of Christ.

From the very beginning God has been showing us that everything we see with our eyes existed first in the spiritual realm and what we are seeing in this natural realm is only a type or a picture of the real thing. This is such a comforting thought. All that we need already exists in a completely perfect and eternal realm and we have been given permission to freely take from this realm, *"Now we have received, not the spirit of the world, but the spirit which is of God; that we might know the things that are freely given to us of God." (1 Cor 2:12 KJV)*

A single eye

The Christian is born into the spiritual realm when he is re-born by the Spirit of God. This means that the Christian must be in tune with the spiritual realm. We are only pilgrims in this natural realm; Heaven is our home. Jesus was only in the natural realm for a short time. The natural realm was not His home.

That is why Paul encourages us to, *"...look not at the things which are seen, but at the things which are not seen: for the things which are seen are temporal; but the things which are not seen are eternal." (2 Pet 1:3 (KJV)*. The things that are seen are the things of this natural realm, which is why they are temporary. The things that are not seen are of the spiritual realm, which is what makes them eternal.

We must not live in such a way that we focus sometimes on the natural realm and at other times on the spiritual realm. The Christian must keep his eyes solely on the things of the spiritual realm that he cannot see, *"The light of the body is the eye: if therefore thine eye be single, thy whole body shall be full of light. But if thine eye be evil, thy whole body shall be full of darkness. If therefore the light that is in thee be darkness, how great is that darkness!" (Matt 6:22-23 KJV)*.

We must have a single eye. We must not flit back and forth between the spiritual realm and the natural realm. I can either focus on what is already existent in the spiritual realm or I can focus on what I am lacking in the natural realm. If I stay focused on my spiritual blessings, my eye is single and my whole body is full of light.

If my eye is not single, the Bible says that it is evil and my whole body is full of darkness. Jesus warns us that if the light we have been given becomes darkness through this wavering practice, it will be a great darkness.

Focus

Just as Jehovah Elohim was able to apprehend the necessary "good" things from the spiritual realm when He needed them, we, through the blood of Jesus can do the very same thing.

Rather than looking at the barren ground that He could see and then complaining about it, Jehovah Elohim looked into the spiritual realm that contained things that couldn't be seen. This is exactly why He apprehended the following from the spiritual realm: A mist, a man, and seeds to plant a garden. As well, rather than looking at the things that *we* can see and complaining them, we must look to the storehouse of spiritual blessings found in the Bible and bring those things that are necessary into this natural realm by faith.

All things exist

We must believe the Bible when it says, *"According as his divine power hath given unto us all things that pertain unto life and godliness..." (2 Pet 1:3 KJV)*. God's divine power "hath", which means "has already", given unto us all things that pertain to life and godliness. Every single thing that we need has already been provided and is waiting to be apprehended from the spiritual realm.

We know all things pertaining to life and godliness exist in the spiritual realm for two reasons: The Bible does not lie and it claims that they exist, and we have not yet witnessed the complete manifestation of them here in the natural realm. These Truths must exist in whole somewhere! The Bible cannot say something that is not true. If we have been given all things pertaining to life and godliness, then those very things must exist in the spiritual realm.

It is much easier to believe for something that the Bible proclaims is already existent than it is to believe for something that still needs to be created. God wants us to know that everything that we could ever possibly need already exists in a timeless and perfect realm.

Faith

With this in mind, the concept of faith becomes much easier to understand, *"Now faith is the substance of things hoped for, the evidence of things not seen. For by it the elders obtained a good report. Through faith we understand that the worlds were framed by the word of God, so that things which are seen were not made of things which do appear." (Heb 11:1-3 KJV).* Faith finds its substance and evidence in the spiritual realm.

Jesus knew

The reason Jesus walked so perfectly and apprehended the things of the spiritual realm so easily is because He had lived in and operated from that realm from everlasting to everlasting. Jesus was there with His Father, creating all things that were necessary for life and godliness in the spiritual realm. Jesus then went on as Jehovah Elohim to tap into these things when the natural realm needed them.

This is why Jesus *the man* knew exactly what to do. Jehovah Elohim is not a stranger to the practice of bringing the spiritual into the natural. Jesus healed, delivered, and worked miracles like He had been doing it forever because He had been doing it for at least four thousand years! Jesus knew how the spiritual realm worked. Jesus never looked at things He saw; He looked at the things of the spiritual realm He could not see with His natural eyes.

When the Bible makes a proclamation that is in contradiction with the natural realm, it is because the Bible is the supernatural Word of God containing the essence of the spiritual realm. We don't need the Bible to tell us what we can see; we need the Bible to tell us about the things we cannot see!

```
The baton has been passed
```

Elohim created everything in the spiritual realm and then sat on His throne and rested. All was created and made in the spiritual realm and Elohim entered a very complete Sabbath rest at the end of this as we read in the culmination of the original creation account.

Elohim, God the Father, is still sitting on His throne; He has not left His rest, *"Thus saith the LORD, The heaven is my throne, and the earth is my footstool: where is the house that ye build unto me? and where is the place of my rest? For all those things hath mine hand made, and all those things have been, saith the LORD..." (Isa 66:1-2a KJV).* God had already made "all those things" and "all those things" already existed. That is why Elohim rests.

Jehovah Elohim took the baton from there and worked with the Holy Spirit and man to begin the process of transferring the necessary things of the spiritual realm into the natural realm. When Jesus died and was resurrected, He went to heaven to join His Father and sit next to Him waiting till His enemies be made His footstool. Jesus has entered God's eternal Sabbath rest.

However, it is evident that there are still things to be apprehended from the spiritual realm. Just as Elohim and Jehovah Elohim had the aid of the Holy Spirit for their tasks, so we have the aid of the Holy Spirit for our task. The baton has been passed to us.

Being buried into Jesus' death and raised by His resurrection, we now walk in the newness of His life, *"...because as he is, so are we in this world." (1 John 4:17b KJV).* We have been invited to enter God's rest and freely receive from the spiritual realm all things necessary for life and godliness.

> In this place I would say a plain word or two to those who understand the method of justification by faith which is in Christ Jesus, but whose trouble is that they cannot cease from sin. We can never be happy, restful, or spiritually healthy till we become holy. We must be rid of sin; but how is the riddance to be wrought? This is the life-or-death question of many. The old nature is very strong, and they have tried to curb and tame it; but it will not be subdued, and they find themselves, though anxious to be better, if anything growing worse than before.
> **All of Grace -- C. H. Spurgeon**

Carnality Calls

There is something in us that rebels against the rules. We have all experienced it, we have all struggled against it, and we have all failed in that struggle.

The minute we go on a diet we become hungry, when we decide to quit smoking we want a cigarette, as soon as we try to quit cursing, we curse more, when we purpose to stop gossiping, we gossip more atrociously than we ever had before, and so on.

Recently, as I was driving in a nearby town I happened to see this sign posted at the entrance to a commercial driveway: **ABSOLUTELY NOT TO BE USED AS A THROUGHWAY.** It was all I could do to not veer left so as to deliberately use this driveway as a throughway. I had no reason to do this; I just wasn't fond of being commanded not to do it.

Why is it that my desire to call people during the day disappears after nine and on the weekends? I shouldn't call them during the day because that would use minutes from my cellular plan. However, calling them after nine and on the weekends is absolutely free! Well, there's no fun in that.

My grandson, who was just vaguely interested in my kitchen cabinets, became ravished with desire to get into these same cabinets the moment I made them off limits. And why is it that we want to do puzzles when they are in the box but not so much when they are sprawled across the dining room table? The dining room table screams to be cleared and we don't like to conform, so we lose interest in the puzzle.

This is the bane of the Christian experience. It seems that we are wired to work contrary to rules, laws, or boundaries of any sort. It doesn't seem to matter whether these regulations are dictated by others, or whether they are self-imposed we are forever falling short of their demands. Our lives bump along from one failure to another always striving and never getting rest. This is the miserable state of all who are born into this world.

The good news is that there is not only a logical, and more importantly, a Biblical *reason* for this utterly miserable state; there is also a logical and Biblical *solution* to it. We are about to discover why we are the way we are. We are going to reveal our "inner sinner", find out where he came from, why he exists, and how to overcome him.

Sin nature

The words "sin nature" do not appear together like this anywhere in the Bible. This term is universally used simply because it describes that defiant part of us. The sin nature is rebellious, lustful, carnal, worldly, and vain. It is all the garbage inside of us that we hate. It is everything with which our born-again spirits disagree. Because it ultimately leads to *sin* and because it is a very real *nature* within us, the term *sin nature* is appropriate.

The "sin nature" is described Biblically in several ways. *Flesh*, *carnality*, *lust*, and *vanity* are the most common of these. The Bible uses these descriptions of the flesh interchangeably, and so will I. The first term we will encounter is "vanity".

Subject to vanity

Our study will begin with Romans 8:20-21. What we will discover in these passages is that God put us under the power, or authority of the sin nature so that He could deliver us from it. God made us prone to sin *on purpose* so that He could rescue us and make us His sons.

We need to understand that, yes, we are failures, but only because that was God's purpose for the opening scene of His drama called "Life". This is very important information concerning our sin nature.

This knowledge takes the air out of the accuser's balloon. The devil loves to throw our sin in our face so that we will run from God and cower in shame until we can muster up enough self-effort to regain audience with Him. This faithless behavior is diametrically opposite to what God had in mind. The devil is a liar.

If God subjected mankind to the sin nature so that He could deliver him from it, then sin should not be a problem for God, or for us. This mindset stops the enemy in his tracks. Sin is all Satan has. If we can remove the problem of sin from the equation, the devil is left with nothing. I believe that is the message of the cross. So, let us study and see if these things be so:

> *"For the creature was made subject to vanity, not willingly, but by reason of him who hath subjected the same in hope, Because the creature itself also shall be delivered from the bondage of corruption into the glorious liberty of the children of God."*
> *(Rom 8:20-21 KJV)*

The King James wording is a little bit choppy, so let's break it down into digestible pieces. It is of utmost importance that we get this message.

"For the creature was made subject to vanity..." In the first chapter of this book we learned that man was first *created* and then *formed*. This particular verse makes this distinction, *"the creature was made."* The Greek word for "creature" is "ktisis" and means, *original formation* and the Greek word for "made subject" is "hupotasso" and means, *to subordinate*. The original creation was subordinated to vanity.

We must consider the original creation of man in the spiritual realm as we read this account. Jehovah Elohim took the original creature from the spiritual realm and then formed him to be in subordination, or subjection to something in the natural. To be subject to something means to be under the authority of it. This "something" is *vanity*. Mankind, the creature was made to be under the authority of *vanity*. Mankind was *created* "good" in the spiritual realm and then he was *formed* in such a way as to be subject to vanity in the natural realm.

The Greek word *vanity* is defined by Strong's Concordance in this way: *moral depravity, excessive pride, futility, worthlessness, something that is considered futile or empty of significance,* and *inutility, which is to be pointless or useless.*

Let's place our definitions within the context of our verse, "The original spiritually created beings were formed in the natural realm in such a way as to be under the authority of moral depravity, pride, futility, worthlessness, insignificance, pointlessness, uselessness." We have just described the sin nature.

Now I get it

Now that we know that mankind was made to be under the authority of a sin nature, we have an explanation for mankind's penchant for failure. How could man possibly do well while being under the authority of depravity, pride, futility, worthlessness, emptiness, and uselessness? It is impossible for one to be good when he is <u>under the power</u> of something that is bad.

From our definitions we can see that the word *vanity* can easily be replaced with the words *sin nature*. Mankind was purposely placed under the power of the sin nature. This explains why we fail the way we do. This is no longer about bad behavior; this is about bad disposition. So why are we bound to this vanity, and who is it that put us in this position?

Is this predicament the "creature's" fault? No, our verses go on to say that the creature was made subject to vanity, *"...not willingly..."* clearly telling us that this condition did not originate in humanity. This word *willingly* is also defined as *voluntarily*. The "creature" did not volunteer for this mission.

Who's the culprit?

If we did not do this to ourselves, it stands to reason that another being did this to us. Someone or something put us, unwillingly, under the authority of the sin nature. Was it the devil? Our verse goes on to expose our subordinator and hint at his plan, *"...but by reason of **him** who has subjected the same..."* Now we have a "him" who had a reason to subject mankind to the sin nature.

As we continue to read, we find both the identity of the "him" and the motivation behind his subjection, *"...in hope, because the creature itself also shall be delivered..."*

Whoever subjected us to the sin nature, did this because he had hope to deliver us. Now it is easy to identify the "Who": God is the only Deliverer. And, it stands to reason that if God is the One with the *reason*, He is also the One Who placed us under the authority of the sin nature.

Out of corruption

As we go on with our verse, we notice that "He" (God) wanted to deliver us, *"...from the bondage of corruption..."* Corruption is decay, ruin, destruction, and death. Corruption is when a good thing goes bad. The use of the word corruption here is different in that it describes the *result* of the sin nature. We had vanity; therefore, we corrupted things. The word *vanity* describes the sin nature, and the word *corruption* describes the ensuing results. God hopes to deliver us from the consequences, or the ensuing results, of our sin nature.

And into liberty

Now that we have learned that God subjected mankind to the sin nature in order to deliver him from corruption, let us go back to our passages to find out what God had in mind when He did this, *"...the creature itself also shall be delivered **into the glorious*** *liberty of the children of God."*

Now we are getting somewhere. If God put us under the authority of something as awful as the sin nature, I'm glad He at least had a glorious plan for us, *"'For I know the plans I have for you," says the LORD. "They are plans for good and not for disaster, to give you a future and a hope.'" (Jer 29:11 NLT).*

So, here's the plan: God subjected us to the sin nature because He hoped to deliver us from the consequences of sin and bring us into the glorious freedom of the children of God.

Wow. It would seem that God laid a net so that He could untangle us, or He dug a ditch so that He could lend us His hand and pull us out. However, at the time that we got caught in that net, or when we fell into that ditch, we were mere men, whereas when we get delivered we will be sons of God. God purposed that we would go from bad, to worse, to better than best! This is so in keeping with the nature of God.

Too good to be bad

As we study this verse, we cannot help but to notice the tone. When speaking of our vanity, or our sin nature, the apostle Paul only speaks of it in relation to God's deliverance.

Let me paraphrase it to help us get a feel for the heart behind the message, *"Although not by their own doing, humans were put under the authority of a sin nature. God had a purpose in this; He hoped to deliver them from the consequences of their sin and bring them into the glorious freedom found in being His children."* There is no arguing, this verse has a good feel to it. Bad news is not being shared. The wording makes it sound like God wanted to take us to a higher place and He purposed to use the sin nature to do it.

If, as is theorized, our sin nature was something we were saddled with because of Adam's sin in the garden, then we are considering the darkest, most evil moment in human history. If that is the case, then why is this bondage to sin talked about in a positive manner?

It wouldn't make sense for God to speak of the sin nature in this manner if it was a curse due to human rebellion. Our verse said we were made subject to this vanity **because He had hope**; *not because humans screwed up.* If our sin nature is a result of human sin, God wouldn't have taken responsibility for it, however, God clearly *does* take responsibility for this bondage. We don't see God complaining about our sin nature; rather He is expressing His hope in the situation. God subjected us to sin because He hoped to deliver us from it.

Which came first: The vanity or the sin?

This is an important question that deserves further attention. Was Adam subjected to the sin nature before he sinned? Is that what caused him to sin? Or, did God curse Adam with a sin nature *after* he sinned? All of humankind has been subject to the sin nature from the beginning, but which beginning? Was the creature made subject to sin at the beginning of Adam's *creation* in the spiritual realm, his *formation* in the natural realm, or at the beginning of his *betrayal*?

The concept of sin couldn't have been present in Adam's creation because God saw His creation and said that it was very good. God does not lie. The sin nature is not "very good" neither can it be called "good" under any circumstances.

Was Adam made subject to sin when Jehovah Elohim formed him in the natural? That is a possibility. If *Adam* was subjected to sin that would mean that mankind had nothing at all to do with the onset of sin.

One who is specifically made to be under the authority of a sin nature will sin regardless of whether or not he wants to. If this theory were true, the burden of responsibility would not fall on mankind. After all, the nature of the beast is what the beast does naturally. If Adam was formed with a sin nature, then the responsibility for Adam's disobedience must fall on God.

Now consider how many times we have heard the following statement: "We would have done the same thing as Adam if we had been the first one created." By universally acknowledging this, what we are saying is that we were all destined to sin. Why is that? Why is it generally accepted that we were all wired for sin, but blasphemous to think that God, *our Maker*, did the wiring?

I don't know how many times I have heard a preacher say, "Aw, we're all stupid. Each one of us would have dropped the ball at some point. We are no different than Adam." We all identify with him; we don't see Adam as the enemy who betrayed all of future mankind by disobeying God.

None of us thinks that if Adam had not eaten of that fruit that everything would have gone along just fine eternally. In our minds, someone was bound to sin. In essence what we are saying is that all humans, made in the image of God were *bound* to sin. And that is exactly what our verse from Romans said.

What we must now do is find out if the sin nature was in existence *before Adam sinned*. If it was, then we should be able to find evidence of it. We should be able to see that sin nature active in the garden if it existed before the first committed sin. This requires that we learn the character of the sin nature. We need to see how the sin nature operates and then look for an indication of it in Adam and Eve before they ate that fruit.

We must be sure about this. After all, if Adam and Eve had a sin nature before they ate that fruit, our doctrines concerning sin must be reevaluated. Essentially, what these verses are telling us is that humankind was bound to sin. That is a hard enough truth to swallow. However, if Adam and Eve were bound as well, we have a whole new ballgame.

The operations of the sin nature

There is a very precise teaching concerning the sin nature in the seventh chapter of Romans. What we will find is that there are three components that come together to cause man to sin: A human, a sin nature, and a law, or commandment (these last two being used interchangeably throughout this text). According to Paul's teaching, all three of these must be present before sin can take place.

The Law

Although I have a sin nature, I have no desire to use driveways as throughways; I needed a law to spark that desire. Before he was forbidden to play in them, my grandson was only mildly interested in playing in my cabinets. After he received the "law", this little one wanted nothing more than to play in those cabinets; he needed a law to spark that longing. Everyone is familiar with this very real aspect of humanity.

Paul tells us that, *"...without the law, sin is dead,"* (Romans 7:8b KJV). Biblically, sin cannot exist without the law. The law must be present in order for sin to be activated, *"...where no law is, there is no transgression."* (Rom 4:15b KJV). So, we see that the law is our first component to sin. The "law" to not use the driveway as a throughway was one component of sin.

The Man

Paul shows us the next component of sin by personalizing this concept and saying that sin gets an opportunity to deceive and kill **him** through the commandment, *"For sin, taking occasion by the* *commandment, deceived **me**, and by it slew **me**." (7:11).*

Sin took an opportunity through the commandment to deceive and kill *him*. I was the "man" who was given the law concerning where to drive. The man is the second component to sin.

The Sin Nature

Paul shows us the final component, *"For we know that the law is spiritual: but I am carnal, sold under sin." (Rom 7:14 KJV)*. The word "carnality" is a Biblical term for the sin nature. Paul admits that the law is spiritual, but this does not help him because he is in bondage to, and under the ownership of the sin nature. Paul is sold under sin. The sin nature within me desired to use the driveway as a throughway simply because it was told not to. The sin nature is the third component to sin.

Is the Law sin?

According to this seventh chapter of Romans, these three elements -- the law, the man, and the sin nature -- combine to produce sin. So is Paul saying that the law is sinful? No, on the contrary, Paul states emphatically that the law is **not** sin: *"Is the law sin? God forbid." (7:7b)*. The law, by itself, is not sin. However sin found an occasion *through* the law to deceive and kill.

Alone, sin is harmless, *"without the law, sin is dead"*, and, alone, the law is harmless, *"Is the law sin? God forbid."*, but man becomes a conductor of sorts through the sin nature, *"I am carnal, sold under sin."* In order for evil to be produced, all three elements must exist. When we put these elements together, the Scriptures say they will deceive and the deception will then kill.

Let there be light!

We will use the example of a lamp to illustrate this point. When one wants to access artificial light, three things are necessary: The lamp, the bulb, and the electricity. When these three come together, they will produce light. If any one of these is missing, there will be no light.

To access sin, three very similar things will be necessary: The man, the law, and the sin nature. The man is likened to a lamp in that he is a vessel, the law is likened to a bulb in that it is "given" to man, and the sin nature is likened to electricity in that it is the "power" within the vessel that enables the sin. When these three come together, they will produce sin. If any one of these in missing, there will be no sin.

So, if the law was not sin, and no sin nature yet existed, where did the "man" Adam get the power to sin? It makes no sense. It is the sin nature, or the vanity to which we were subjected which causes us to sin. So let's do a test to find out if Adam had this sin nature *before* his original sin. We will put a "bulb" in pre-sin Adam to see if he lights.

Jehovah Elohim put a bulb in Adam when He gave him the commandment to not eat of the forbidden fruit. When this law was "plugged into" Adam, he sinned. The light came on. There was a law and there was a man, and since the result was sin, there must also have been a sin nature.

Adam *did* have the power to sin when the law was plugged into him, *"For I was alive without the law once: but when the commandment came, sin revived, and I died." (Rom 7:9).* Paul spoke these words concerning the sin nature; nonetheless, doesn't it sound like Adam could have spoken them?

Forbidden Fruit

To understand the properties of the law when it mixes with the sin nature, let us consider the fact that God gave Adam only one law. Not only was sin the result when this commandment came, but

Adam broke the only law he was given. If God didn't want sin, all He had to do was withhold any and all laws, *"without the law, sin is dead."* God knew that.

I'm sure Adam didn't eat of the forbidden fruit because he was starving. I am equally sure he had several varieties of delicious fruits that were quite permissible for him to eat. I don't care what that serpent had to say, a rational man who is walking a life of perfection with God is not going to give in to the temptation to rebel against his God by unnecessarily eating a piece of fruit!

But was Adam a rational man? I, personally, know all about the sin nature and there is nothing rational about it. To even think about using a driveway as a throughway solely because I was told not to is irrational. There are times when I want to step out of my body just so that I can give myself a strange look.

Adam was given a law that awakened an evil inside of him that he didn't even know existed. He ate of that forbidden fruit because he could do no other. Adam was created in the image of God and he was a magnificent creation, but due to how he was formed in the natural, he was not dealing with a full deck.

A longing for that which is forbidden

Adam and Eve sinned because they had a sin nature that empowered them to sin. Going back to the seventh chapter of Romans, we can see this sin nature in action as Paul says, *"For the good that I would I do not: but the evil which I would not, that I do." (Rom 7:19 KJV).*

Paul says that the very things he wants to do he doesn't do, but the evil that he does not want to do is what he actually does! Notice that something is drawing Paul in the opposite direction of the law, *"But sin, taking occasion by the commandment, wrought in me all manner of concupiscence. For without the law sin was dead."*

(Rom 7:8 KJV). The word *wrought* means *to work fully*. The word concupiscence is defined as lust: A longing for that which is forbidden. Sin gained an opportunity through the law to work in man a lust for that which was forbidden.

Paul goes so far as to say, *"What shall we say then? Is the law sin? God forbid. I had not known sin, but by the law: for I had not known lust, except the law had said, Thou shalt not covet." (Rom 7:7 KJV)*. Paul would not have known he had a nature that longed for that which was forbidden, if he had not been given a law that was forbidding something. (You might need to read that over once or twice.) Now Paul is beginning to understand his wretchedness.

Drawn away

The book of James explains how sin comes about, *"But every man is tempted, when he is drawn away of his own lust, and enticed. (James 1:14 KJV)*. This lust, (a longing for that which is forbidden), is powerful stuff. Romeo and Juliet were perfect examples of the compelling force of forbidden fruit.

Most don't know this, but Juliet was not Romeo's first love; she was his rebound love. Romeo and Juliet's lust to be together was not fueled by a remarkable love; it was fuelled by their families' commands to stay away from each other.

Lust is not a longing for things that are *desired;* it is a longing that specifically longs for things that have been forbidden. Romeo and Juliet's lust, fueled by the "law" of their parents, was so strong that it empowered them to take their own lives.

What I like about our verses from James is that they say that man is *drawn away* of his own lust. The words "drawn away" actually mean to *drag forth*. This verse is saying that our own lust drags us toward sin. This is another indication of the sin nature. We aren't *willingly* going toward sin; it is the lust within us that is dragging us toward it.

One need not be *dragged away* to temptation unless one initially does not want to go. If we *wanted* to sin, we would not have to be dragged to it; we would just go there willingly, *"For I delight in the law of God after the inward man: But I see another law in my members, warring against the law of my mind, and bringing me into captivity to the law of sin which is in my members." (Rom 7:22-23 KJV).*

According to Paul, there is a very real struggle taking place. Paul wants to go one direction, however, his lust is drawing him in the opposite direction, and *"The creature was subject to vanity, not willingly"*

We don't lust because we want to. None of us wants to have a sin nature. Nonetheless, there is something inside of us that desires things that are forbidden. Adam and Eve were shackled to this very thing; their lustful sin nature longed for that forbidden fruit.

Born to be wild

When we think about it, giving in to lust is the most direct act of rebellion known to man. When an authority points us in one direction and we go the opposite, we are saying that we are the authority and we will make the rules.

When Adam disobeyed God he was usurping His throne. Adam put himself higher than the Most High. God pointed to the permitted fruit and Adam did an about face and made a B-line to the forbidden fruit. In doing this, Adam put himself in the place of God and broke the very first commandment that commands that we not have any gods before Him. This is a big deal.

Apparently, God made us in such a way that we would be forcefully compelled to defy Him and try to be our own gods. That is the essence of the sin nature. And when we look around, we see that humanity is clearly locked into this.

The Bible says we are drawn away of our own lust. There is something inside of us that pulls us away from God, places us on our own throne, and pits us against Him. God gave Himself the greatest challenge simply because He was up to it. God has every intention and the wherewithal to deliver us from this contrary nature. In fact, it was God's purpose to deliver us. He is, after all, the omnipotent God.

Did Adam have lust?

We looked for a sin nature in Adam and found one. Just to make sure we are on the right track, let's look for the progression of lust in Adam according to our verses from James, *"But every man is tempted, when he is drawn away of his own lust, and enticed. Then when lust hath conceived, it bringeth forth sin: and sin, when it is finished, bringeth forth death." (James 1:14-16 KJV).*

The first thing I notice is that after a man is drawn away of his own lust, he is enticed. To "entice" means to trap or delude. James has just described how man sins: He is tempted when he is drawn away by his longing for that which is forbidden, enticed by the devil, and trapped. This sounds precisely like what happened to Adam and Eve.

But what lust did Adam and Eve have? They *lusted* to eat the fruit since that is the only thing they were forbidden to do. That is the nature of lust; a longing for that which is forbidden. We will see this lust in action as the story unfolds.

They were drawn away

The lust to eat the fruit drew Adam and Eve away, which explains why Adam and Eve were in the vicinity of the tree of knowledge of good and evil and not in the presence of God. Adam and Eve were drawn away.

I'm sure the Garden of Eden was very large. Why else would the man and the woman be hanging out in the only place they could get in trouble? They were *"drawn away of their own lust"* and according to James, that's the first step. Adam and Eve were drawn away from God by their lust for the forbidden fruit.

Enticed

Once they were drawn away, then they were enticed. Notice where the serpent had positioned himself: The Tree. The devil knew Adam and Eve would eventually come; he was probably filing his nails. The devil plays a very important roll in this drama.

Once Adam and Eve got to the tree, Satan was in a position to entice, *"...Yea, hath God said, Ye shall not eat of every tree of the garden?" (Gen 3:1 KJV)*. You see, the Greek root word for "entice" means to throw down bait. Evidently the devil knew that the law was the perfect bait to cast when fishing for sin. He was right.

Temptation

Next we see the actual temptation, *"Go ahead and eat; ye shall not surely die." (paraphrase)*. It is the devil's job to try to tempt us through his lies. God gives us Truth and the devil follows this by giving us lies. Because we have a lusting sin nature that pulls us away from God, our natural response is to fall prey to these lies.

Lust is conceived

When Eve was enticed to disobey the law, her lust exposed itself, *"... the woman saw that the tree was good for food, and that it was pleasant to the eyes, and a tree to be desired to make one wise..."* Do we think that this particular tree was more beautiful than all the others? Of course not. We're talking about the Garden of Eden! I think it is safe to say that all the trees were good for food and pleasant to the eyes. However, the Tree of Knowledge of Good and Evil seemed *especially* good and pleasant. Adam and Eve were drawn away; Eve was then enticed, and finally tempted.

Sin comes forth

Now the lust for that fruit is conceived, *"...she took of the fruit thereof, and did eat, and gave also unto her husband with her; and he did eat." (Gen 3:6 KJV)*.

Sin conceived and brought forth death

God does not mince words. God had told Adam and Eve, *"But of the tree of the knowledge of good and evil, thou shalt not eat of it: for in the day that thou eatest thereof thou shalt surely die." (Gen 2:17 KJV)*. Therefore, immediately after Adam and Eve ate the forbidden fruit, God asked Eve, *"What is this that thou hast done?"* Eve answered Him, *"...The serpent beguiled me, and I did eat." (Gen 3:13 KJV)*.

There was no further discussion as God proceeded to curse the devil, the man, and the woman. This curse brought death into humanity just as God had predicted, *"Wherefore, as by one man sin entered into the world, and death by sin; and so death passed upon all men, for that all have sinned:" (Rom 5:12 KJV)*.

Perfectly deadly progression

Adam and Eve should be the picture next to the definition of lust. When we break down the wording of our verse from James, *"But every man is tempted, when he is drawn away of his own lust, and enticed. Then when lust hath conceived, it bringeth forth sin: and sin, when it is finished, bringeth forth death."*, we can see how the actions of Adam and Eve followed suit:

1. *"Every man..."*: Adam and Eve
2. *"...is tempted..."*: "...Ye shall not surely die"
3. *"...when he is drawn away..."*: Drawn to the tree.
4. *"...of his own lust..."*: A longing for the forbidden fruit.
5. *"...and enticed..."*: "...Yea, hath God said, Ye shall not eat of every tree of the garden?"
6. *"...Lust hath conceived..."*: "the woman saw that the tree was good, pleasant, and desirous..."
7. *"...it bringeth forth sin..."*: "she took of the fruit thereof, and did eat, and gave also unto her husband with her; and he did eat."
8. *"...when it is finished, bringeth forth death"*: Sin entered and death was passed on to all men... *"cursed is the ground for thy sake...till thou return unto the ground for out of it wast thou taken: for dust thou art, and unto dust shalt thou return."*

Hence it becomes more than obvious that Adam and Eve had a sin nature that filled them with lust. They fit the pattern exactly.

No Law; no sin

This explains how it is that Adam and Eve were able to walk a perfect, sinless life before they ate of the fruit. Even as a Christian, I don't know if I could pull off even one perfect day. Adam, in particular, pulled off perfection for an enormous amount of time, only to fail at this one very simple task.

Consider the fact that in the second chapter of Genesis, there was no plant life at all until God made the man and placed him in the garden. It was after this that, *"...out of the ground made the LORD God to grow every tree that is pleasant to the sight, and good for food; the tree of life also in the midst of the garden, and the tree of knowledge of good and evil." (Gen 2:9 KJV)*.

I do not believe, as do some, that God made the plant life grow instantly into mature fruit bearing plants. God obeys His own rules. If trees take several years to produce fruit now, then trees took several years to produce fruit then. These trees and plants were part of the natural realm; therefore they grew naturally.

When Moses (the author of Genesis) commented as to why the land was barren in the first place, he did not use the explanation that God hadn't yet provided that "miracle". Rather, he said, *"for the LORD God had not caused it to rain upon the earth, and there was not a man to till the ground." (Gen 2:6 KJV)*. We are given the reason why the earth had not sprung forth vegetation.

This shows us that God planned on using *natural* as opposed to *supernatural* methods to cause His garden to grow. From the very beginning God purposed that weather and mankind would work together to produce fruit bearing plant life. And that is why when Jehovah Elohim saw barren ground He promptly provided the water and the man.

The introduction of mist and man did not instantaneously produce mature fruit bearing plants. What the addition of man and mist *did* produce was the natural method of gardening. Now that a man was tilling the ground and a mist was watering the ground, the seeds that were sown into the ground by Jehovah Elohim were now able to germinate, spring forth, and grow, *"And out of the ground made the LORD God to grow…"*

As Adam tended that garden, the trees began to grow. If the Tree of Knowledge of Good and Evil was mature enough to be bearing fruit, it had to be several years old. What this tells us is that Adam walked without sinning for several years, *"And the LORD God **planted** a garden eastward in Eden; and there he put the man whom he had formed."*

No other law to break

Adam walked in perfection only to break the exact law he was given because he knew of no other law to break. All the other laws were encapsulated in the Tree of Knowledge of Good and Evil. I believe the only reason it took Adam and Eve so long to finally eat that fruit is because it took exactly that long for the fruit to develop. Once the tree had juicy, ripe fruit, Adam and Eve were compelled toward it by the lust that was within them, *"Every man is tempted when he is drawn away and enticed..."*

Had God commanded Adam to not murder Eve, Adam probably would have murdered her! The law that forbad murder would have awoken Adam's lust that longed for things forbidden. This sin would have manifested just as the sin of eating that fruit manifested. Once humankind was opened up to all knowledge of good and evil it only took *one* generation to activate the law that forbad murder, *"Cain rose up against Abel his brother, and slew him." (Gen 4:8).*

The law that God gave Adam was the same law that empowered his sin. Adam and Eve did not lie, cheat, or steal, because God did not give them laws concerning these things. The specific law that God gave Adam and Eve rubbed them the wrong way, so to speak. Nothing else was forbidden; hence, nothing else awakened their lust.

It was the command to *not eat of the tree* that the serpent was able to use to entice that sin nature. If this is not true, then we are being asked to accept the world's biggest coincidence: Adam and Eve just happened to break the only law they were given? Hardly.

Predisposed to Sin

Evidently, Adam *was* predisposed to sin. Being now convinced of this, we must face the facts: God purposely made Adam in such a way that Adam had no choice but to sin. Adam did not screw up God's plan. God did not go into a panic and try to think of plan "B". No...plan "A" was coming along rather well. You see,

Adam did exactly what God knew he would do and what He purposed him to do.

God did not skip a beat in getting victory over Adam's sin as He doled out the devil's curse, *"And I will put enmity between thee and the woman, and between thy seed and her seed; it shall bruise thy head, and thou shalt bruise his heel." (Gen 3:15 KJV).* Complete victory over sin is found in this verse. In pronouncing His curse on man, God set up the earth in such a way that mankind would be in constant need of a Deliverer.

"For the creature was made subject to vanity, not willingly, but by reason of him who hath subjected the same in hope, Because the creature itself also shall be delivered from the bondage of corruption into the glorious liberty of the children of God."

It was God's will for Adam to sin. This changes our doctrine tremendously. We can no longer claim that Adam was a fool and that by association we are all fools. Adam was not foolish; he was simply hell bent from the get-go.

Yes, we have to accept the fact that we are wretched, worthless, and useless, but who says we have to take the blame for it? Paul didn't take the blame for his sin. Paul specifically said that he was a prisoner of sin. He accepted his bondage, received deliverance from it, and then moved on (Romans 7). We will speak much more of this in a later book.

Nothing noteworthy

Have you noticed that the story of mankind did not begin to get recorded until Adam sinned? We know next to nothing about pre-sin Adam. Now that we know that Adam walked in perfect communion with God for several years, why do we not have great stories about this so called "amazing" life? Was there nothing noteworthy? God makes Adam, Adam names the animals, God creates Eve, time goes by, more time goes by (I can almost hear God whistling), and then Adam sins. Okay, now we can go on with the story.

Add to this the fact that Adam and Eve did not begin to replenish the earth until after they had sinned. This is sure-fire evidence that God was not going to go on with the story of man until man ate of that forbidden fruit! The plot was at a standstill until that moment in time when all hell would break loose according to God's original plan.

We know that God has His reasons for doing the things that He does. For now, it is enough for us to relax and realize that we are not self-made idiots who get our kicks out of defying God. Simply put, God had a plan and, evidently, the sin nature played a key role.

`"I create evil"`

We can no longer look at our sin the same way. We must embrace the idea that our sin natures are God imposed. Jehovah Elohim formed us in such a way that we would have no choice but to sin. Now we can better understand Passages such as the following:

"I am the LORD, and there is none else, there is no God beside me: I girded thee, though thou hast not known me: That they may know from the rising of the sun, and from the west, that there is none beside me. I am the LORD, and there is none else. ***I form the light, and create darkness: I make peace, and create evil:*** *I the LORD do all these things." (Isa 45:5-7 KJV emphasis mine).*

God emphatically states that He is in control. Period. God goes on to say that He is the One Who creates darkness and evil *as well as* light and peace. God is the essence of all good; however He created darkness and evil. God purposed to use darkness and evil with mankind, *"The creature was subject to vanity, not willingly..."*

We don't question Him

We must not strive with God over the idea that He created evil and used it in His plan with man. God knew people would have a hard time with this, which is why just four verses later He offers this adamant retort, *"Woe to him who strives with his Maker! Let the potsherd strive with the potsherds of the earth! Shall the clay say to him who forms it, 'What are you making?' Or shall your handiwork say, 'He has no hands'? Woe to him who says to his father, 'What are you begetting?' Or to the woman, 'What have you brought forth?'"* (Isa 45:9-10 NKJV).

This verse gives reference to a forming, a making, a working, a birthing and a bringing forth, but not a creating. Elohim created a perfect being; Jehovah Elohim fashioned and birthed a man who was hell bent. How wonderful that we can be born again!

When the Bible teaches us a Truth that may be hard to swallow, we must not question God's methods. Jehovah Elohim is the Potter; we are simply the clay. It is understandable that we would balk at this news; He obviously knew that we would which is why He instructs us to not forget that He is God and He will do what He sees fit with these bodies of ours, regardless of what we think about it.

Don't miss the message

We cannot miss the message of these verses. By saying, "Don't question Me about how I made you.", God is saying that He fully expects us to wonder why He made us the way He did. Had God formed us perfectly, we would have no reason to question how He formed us and this would have been an unnecessary verse. But, God did *not* form us perfect, rather He formed us in a way that *would* be disagreeable to us. When we first come to this realization, we will naturally have questions.

However, we are sternly told to not question. This admonition teaches me two things concerning the way Jehovah Elohim formed me: It is done and I have to deal with it, and if God did it, He must have had a good reason and I need not be anxious about it.

My natural father is a strong authoritarian. We were never allowed to question him. Some may not agree with this sort of parenting, but it had value. I was comforted by the fact that my father was in control; he was not wishy-washy. My father knew what he was doing, he believed it to be right, and he really didn't care whether or not I agreed with him. He was the father and that was the end of the conversation. It is easy to rest and feel safe when someone is unquestioningly in control.

So, when my Father in heaven says, "I made you the way I made you, now don't question Me.", this helps me to safely enter into His rest knowing that God is in control and knows what He is doing. I can take comfort in this and simply accept my sin situation as a fact and rest assured that God has a remedy. After all, He is God and He can do whatever He would like; He affords Himself complete creative license.

We must accept the fact that this is the reality we have been given. Sin had a place in humanity. Bondage to sin was not our idea, and it is not our fault, but it is our problem. And since we are in this thing with the Answer to all problems, as the saying goes, *"everything is gonna be all right."*

Free to be Holy

The heart is so hard, the will is so obstinate, the passions are so furious, the thoughts are so volatile, the imagination is so ungovernable, the desires are so wild, that the man feels that he has a den of wild beasts within him, which will eat him up sooner than be ruled by him. We may say of our fallen nature what the Lord said to Job concerning Leviathan: "Wilt thou play with him as with a bird? or wilt thou bind him for thy maidens?"
All of Grace, C. H. Spurgeon

Hell Dust

Once I learned that Adam's sin nature was built into him, I wanted to know where it came from. We know that Elohim created man *good* in the spiritual realm, but how did Jehovah Elohim form him in the natural?

We are going to study the creation account once again and find out what Jehovah Elohim did to put His man in a position to be delivered.

Just after Elohim created the heavens and the earth in the first verse of the Bible, He gave the following description of the earth, as it is recorded in Genesis, *"And the earth was **without form**, and **void**; and **darkness** was upon the face of the **deep**. And the Spirit of God moved upon the face of the waters." (Gen 1:2 KJV emphasis mine)*. This is quite a description. I will use the Strong's concordance to Biblically define the main words in our verse, which I have placed in bold face.

- **Without form:** *to lie waste; a desolation (of surface), that is, desert; a worthless thing; in vain:—confusion, empty place, without form, nothing, (thing of) nought, vain, vanity, waste, wilderness.*
- **Void:** *(meaning to be empty); a vacuity, that is, an undistinguishable ruin:—emptiness, void.*
- **Darkness:** *the dark; hence darkness; misery, destruction, death, ignorance, sorrow, wickedness:—dark (-ness), night, obscurity.*
- **Deep:** *an abyss (as a surging mass of water), especially the deep (the main sea or the subterranean water supply):—deep (place), depth.*

Without form and void

To begin our study in this second verse of the Bible, we find that the words *without form* and this particular form of the word *void* are used <u>just one other time in the Bible</u>. Together, their equivalents make up the Hebrew phrase "tohu bohu". Interestingly, these words describing the state of the earth in Genesis *also* speak of the great wrath of God upon Jerusalem and Judah in the book of Jeremiah. The following is almost word for word, *"I beheld the earth, and, lo, it was without form, and void;*

and the heavens, and they had no light." (Jer 4:23 KJV).

In this fourth chapter of Jeremiah, God begins by blasting Jerusalem and Judah for their many abominable acts. With fierce anger God listed their sins, *"For my people is foolish, they have not known me; they are sottish children, and they have none understanding: they are wise to do evil, but to do good they have no knowledge. I beheld the earth, and, lo, it was without form, and void; and the heavens, and they had no light" (Jer 4:22-23 KJV).*

God proceeds to describe the wrath He is bringing to destroy Jerusalem and Judah, *"I beheld the mountains, and, lo, they trembled, and all the hills moved lightly. I beheld, and, lo, there was no man, and all the birds of the heavens were fled. I beheld, and, lo, the fruitful place was a wilderness, and all the cities thereof were broken down at the presence of the LORD, and by his fierce anger." (Jer 4:24-26 KJV).* So, this particular word grouping is found only twice throughout the entire Bible; once to describe terrible retribution from God, and once to describe the state of the earth as the Holy Spirit first moved upon it.

Again, the words "without form and void" (tohu bohu) mean *to lie waste, a desolation, a worthless thing, confusion, vanity, undistinguishable ruin, emptiness, void.* Interestingly, our definition includes the word *vanity*; the very thing to which we were subjected. If you remember, the word vanity was defined as, *moral depravity, excessive pride, futility, worthlessness, something that is considered futile or empty of significance.* These two meanings are notably similar.

Darkness

As we study the Hebrew word for darkness, I will give you the definitions as I found them. I just gave the gist of each of the meanings. There are six different words in the Hebrew dictionary that are translated into the word "darkness". These are the five

God chose **not** to use when describing the earth in Genesis:

H6205: cloudy
H653: Misfortune and concealment
H3990: opaque
H5890: covering
H4285: a dark place

Although none of these definitions paint a cheery picture, they are mere child's play when compared to the definition of the word God *did* choose to use to describe the earth in Genesis:

H2822 choshek: *dark; darkness; misery, destruction, death, ignorance, sorrow, wickedness:—night, obscurity.* Now that's dark -- in every sense of the word!

Deep

When we look at the word *deep*, we find 5 definitions. Four of them define a deep place, and two speak specifically of water in a very calming sense. But consider what word was chosen to describe the state of the waters upon the earth: *t^{e}hom*, meaning, *An abyss (as a surging mass of water), especially the deep (the main sea or the subterranean water supply):—deep (place), depth.*

When speaking of the depth of the water, the word, *t^{e}hom* is the only one that speaks of a *subterranean* depth. The word *hell* is Biblically defined as a **subterranean** retreat.

In addition to this, we find that we have an *abysmal surging mass of water*. So, whatever happened to the earth to cause it to be in a state of misery, destruction, sorrow, and wickedness, impacted it so severely that the great masses of waters were disturbed. The root word in this word *deep* (t^{e}hom), is "hum": *to make an uproar, or agitate greatly:—destroy, move, make a noise,...* So the particular word that was translated "deep" was taken directly from a root word meaning *to make an uproar and agitate greatly*.

So why were the deeps of the water disturbed? Why were they not placid? There was no weather as of yet; weather is produced by sun and moon, which had not yet been created. But, nevertheless, what is described to us in Genesis is a surging mass of water.

A disturbance

Something has caused a great disturbance. A body of water will remain placid unless something disturbs it. Water does not, in and of itself, surge around. If that water was surging, something must have happened to cause it to surge. And, since this occurrence is found in the very same verse as the hideous description of the earth, we must draw the conclusion that the one had something to do with the other.

Let's review the specific descriptive words used to give a depiction of the state of the earth when the Holy Spirit moved upon it in the first chapter of Genesis: *Waste, desolation, worthless thing, confusion, wilderness, void, indistinguishable ruin, darkness, misery, destruction, death, sorrow, ignorance, wickedness, obscurity, and an abysmal, surging mass of water.*

An indistinguishable ruin

Is it just me, or does this sound like hell? Physically and metaphorically this is a description of hell. I find it absolutely fascinating that the Holy Spirit was moving upon the face of an indistinguishable ruin. Indistinguishable? How bad was it? When I think of an indistinguishable ruin, I think of the aftermath of a nuclear bomb or a natural disaster such as a tornado or a hurricane.

One would think the Holy Spirit of God would do one of two things as He saw the earth in such a condition: Either make a B-line to another planet, or clean up this one before He decides to make man upon it. But, that is not what He does.

Let there be light

Rather than changing or fixing anything, God immediately addressed the hellish situation, *"And God said, Let there be light: and there was light. And God saw the light, that it was good: and God divided the light from the darkness. And God called the light Day, and the darkness he called Night. And the evening and the morning were the first day." (Gen 1:3-5 KJV).*

By this description, it is easy to assume that this is when God created the sun. But upon further study, we find that God clearly created the sun and the moon on the *fourth* day of creation, not the first day *(Gen 1:14-18 KJV).*

The light which God created on that first day was the opposite of what presently existed on the earth which is why He divided the one from the other. To an earth full of death, destruction, misery, and darkness, God brought life, creation, goodness and light. God brought to earth the other end of the spectrum; He then divided the two.

The Light of Truth

The word that best defines the light that was brought to earth on that first day of creation is *illumination*. God spoke into being the kind of light which is described in the New Testament, *"Ye are all the children of light, and the children of the day: we are not of the night, nor of darkness." (1Thes 5:5).* Notice this verse refers to light and darkness as day and night just as in Genesis. When we read the chapter that contains this verse, we find that light is Truth and goodness whereas darkness is lies and evil.

On that first day, God spoke into being a spiritual light that stood in stark contrast to the darkness and evil that presently pervaded the earth. This is the very thing to which Jesus was referring when He gave instructions to Paul, *"To open their eyes, and to turn them from darkness to light, and from the power of Satan unto God..." (Acts 26:18a).* Jesus was commissioning Paul to convert troops from the devil's side to God's side, from darkness to light, from night to day. Paul did this very well and his writings continue to do this every day.

`Darkness could not reside in heaven`

For all we know, this may have been the first time in history that good and evil, light and dark, and day and night resided together. We know from Scripture that God did now allow evil in heaven. We read in Isaiah that the devil, or Lucifer, was cast from heaven when evil was found in him, *"Thou wast perfect in thy ways from the day that thou wast created, till iniquity was found in thee....How art thou **fallen from heaven**, O Lucifer, son of the morning! how art thou cut down to the ground, which didst weaken the nations!" (Ezek 28:15 & Isa 14:12 KJV emphasis mine).*

Jesus refers to this verse when describing Satan, *"And he said unto them, I beheld Satan as lightning fall from heaven." (Luke 10:18 KJV).* According to Ezekiel, Satan got into pride, *"Thine heart was lifted up because of thy beauty, thou hast corrupted thy wisdom by reason of thy brightness...",* and then he was cast down, *"I will cast thee to the ground, I will lay thee before kings, that they may behold thee." (28:17 KJV).*

By casting Lucifer from heaven, we can see that God wouldn't allow evil to take up its home in heaven. Why then is God perfectly fine with allowing it to exist in the earth with His creation? Keep in mind that God did not cast the evil darkness away; He introduced light, and then He separated the two.

Although He would not allow evil to reside in heaven, God did allow this indistinguishable ruin and misery to continue on the earth. Evil and darkness have a significant purpose on God's earth.

Earth is Hell

If Lucifer was cast from his position in heaven, where was he thrown? We know that at the time of creation the devil was on earth as we saw him in the Garden. Additionally, Isaiah, while giving the account of Lucifer's betrayal and subsequent demise, says this, *"Hell from beneath is moved for thee to meet thee at thy coming:" (Isa 14:9a).* According to the Hebrew definition, hell was violently quaking in fear and anger as it anticipated Lucifer's impact.

If Lucifer's first stop was hell, I'm pretty sure it was also his last stop. I don't think Satan was banished to some "hell" planet and was then released to earth. We also have proof that hell is in the heart of the earth through the words of Jesus, *"For as Jonas was three days and three nights in the whale's belly; so shall the Son of man be three days and three nights in the heart of the earth." (Matt 12:40 KJV).*

So when we take our hellish description of earth from the second verse of Genesis, add to it the fact that Lucifer was thrown to hell, and then consider that he was roaming around on earth during the time of Adam and Eve, we can only draw one conclusion: Earth is hell and that is precisely why Satan is here.

We will speak more of earth being hell in a later chapter. For now it is enough to understand that the *face* of the earth, though it be a portion of hell, is *not* the place of departed souls or eternal damnation.

No wonder

So, Satan was thrown to earth, which, at some point, became *"hell from beneath moving for Satan to meet him at his coming."* Now we can understand why earth was in such a state. I can't imagine what kind of impact Satan made in the earth when all that rebellious, prideful evil was cast from the heaven by the powerful hand of God.

Casting Lucifer to earth was God's way of "casting" him as the lead antagonist in this drama called "Life". God is the great Protagonist being the epitome of good whereas Satan, through his rebellion, instantly became the antagonist of all that is good. As he was ejected from heaven, Lucifer's connection to the God of love and life was forever severed. Nothing but a festering ball of diabolical evil, death, and destruction, Satan careened toward earth fueled by the blast of God's anger.

Look out below!

Meteors that break through our atmosphere are then pulled by gravity toward earth as fireballs from the sky. When they make contact, they produce large craters. The "deep" or the abyss that is spoken of in Genesis was probably an enormous hole that was created at the point of Satan's impact. We could call this crater ground zero. The fallout from this catastrophic collision probably covered the earth just as would the fallout from a large meteor.

When Satan hit the earth, the ground was pulverized and propelled upwards into the atmosphere forming a mushroom cloud. As the ash rained down, darkness hung like a cloak. The waters were surging due to this great geological disturbance.

After shaking off the dust, the devil began to ascend from his pit. The first thing He saw when his dark eyes emerged above the rim of his abyss was the same thing the Spirit of God saw when he moved upon the face of the earth: An indescribable ruin. Welcome home.

When we consider this scenario, our description of the earth in Genesis seems quite fitting.

It was all in the material

What about man? How exactly did evil taint man? It was all in the material: God made a perfectly good man out of perfectly hellish material.

We have already studied the fact that God, Elohim, created all things good in the spiritual realm during the first week of creation. When we studied the second chapter of Genesis we found that Jehovah Elohim *formed* these same creations in the natural realm. It was in the forming of man in the natural realm that he was formed of the dust of the earth.

To get a better understanding, let's consider the result if one were to get a hold of a world class recipe for brownies and choose to use poisoned flour to make them. It would not matter if the directions were followed exactly, the end result would be deadly.

When the brownies come out of the oven, they will look good, smell good, and they may even taste good, however, being poisoned through the flour, they will be deadly. Although the brownies were created "good", they were formed out of bad stuff. Elohim had a good "recipe" in mankind; He created man good and in His image. Nevertheless, what kind of flour did *Jehovah* Elohim use to make those brownies in the natural realm?

The dust of the earth

In the second chapter of Genesis, we read that God *formed* the plant life, the animal kingdom, and Adam and Eve. God made all living beings out of a material, *"And the LORD God formed man of the **dust** of the ground...And out of the **ground** made the LORD God to grow every tree...And out of the **ground** the LORD God* *formed every beast of the field, and every fowl of the air..." (Gen 2:7&9a &19a emphasis mine).* Jehovah Elohim used materials to form His living creations.

What drew my attention was the fact that the plant and animal life were made out of the *ground* while Adam, the human, was made out of the *dust* of the ground. This prompted me to do another word study.

The Hebrew word for "ground" is *adamah* and simply means *soil.* But the Hebrew word for "dust" is *aphar* and means *dust (as powdered or gray); hence clay, earth, mud:—ashes, dust, ground, morter, powder, rubbish...to be gray or perhaps rather to pulverize; to be dust:—cast [dust].* Clearly, this is a different word.

Why would God make the plants and animals from *ground* and the first human from the *dust* of the ground? I could understand if God had made the human from a *better* substance, but when we consider the definitions, we see that the dust of the ground appears to be a lower form of material than that of the ground.

What is this dust?

This particular word, aphar (dust) is used sparingly in the Bible. Aphar is most commonly used *metaphorically* when illustrating the concept of "a lot", *"And I will make thy seed as the dust of the earth: so that if a man can number the dust of the earth, then shall thy seed also be numbered." (Gen 13:16 KJV).* However, other than using *aphar* to give the idea of a large number, the word *aphar* is only used in a negative sense.

It is in the *concrete* usage of the word that we find the negative connotation. Here are just a few of the examples I found of the word, aphar; the dust of which man was made: As part of his punishment for tempting Adam and Eve, Satan was made to eat aphar dust all the days of his life (Gen 3:14). The aphar dust of the land became lice in Egypt (Ex 8:16). Aphar dust was used many times in sacrifices for sins (Numbers). It was the practice of the Israelites, and still is today, to put aphar dust upon their heads during times of great mourning or to denote grave regret.

As well, aphar dust is commonly used in judgment and wrath, *"The LORD shall make the rain of thy land powder and dust: from heaven shall it come down upon thee, until thou be destroyed." (Deut 28:24 KJV).*

For example, when the children of Israel rebelled against God and made a golden calf while Moses was on the mount, Moses took the calf which they had made and burned it and ground it to dust and made the children of Israel drink of it. When referring to this incidence in the book of Deuteronomy, Moses described this powder using *aphar* as the word for dust. In the Book of Nehemiah, the word aphar is translated as "rubbish".

The thing we need to notice is that although the word *ground* is used in a great many positive senses, the word aphar is never used in a positive sense. Man was formed of the *dust* of the earth. Jehovah Elohim chose to form man with a material that, in its concrete form, is only used in a negative sense. Dust is probably the most worthless substance on earth. This is why the Israelites use aphar dust to convey the message of worthlessness in times of repentance.

Hell Dust

So, where did this dust come from? Very large explosions, which are caused when two objects collide, can pulverize one or both objects and result in fallout of dust or ash. We saw it with the nuclear bombs used against Japan in World War II. We saw it when a jet collided with a building causing it to crash down upon itself on 9/11. We already spoke of how a meteor colliding with earth will produce dust or ash.

Was the dust from which we were formed nothing more than the fallout ash from the crater that was produced by the impact of Satan upon the earth when he was cast from heaven? Is this the raw material God chose when making Adam? Yes, I believe God used the very dust that was produced when evil rebellion collided with the earth and left it an indistinguishable ruin. That is why one of our definitions of this dust (aphar) means *to pulverize*.

A cataclysmic impact is the only explanation for why there would even *be* dust on the earth. We know the earth was not dust; it was ground. And we know the ground was not dust; it was earth. When we step outside, we do not see dust unless something has specifically caused dirt to be somehow turned into dust. There simply is no explanation as to why dust was on the earth, which is why I favor the idea of a cataclysmic impact; it is the only lead we have.

God used this dust

I believe the ash that remained after Satan's impact is the very dust of which we were made. This theory makes sense. Consider what David said, *"Like as a father pitieth his children, so the LORD pitieth them that fear him. For he knoweth our frame; he remembereth that we are* (aphar) *dust." (Psa 103:13-14 KJV parentheses mine).*

God likens Himself to a Father Who pities His children. The word *pities* means to be compassionate. Just like a father who is compassionate with his children so the Lord is compassionate with those who fear Him. A father is compassionate with his children because he knows that they are imperfect. God is compassionate with us because He knows that we are imperfect.

God knows our *frame*. In Hebrew this means that God knows our *forming*. The root word for "frame" means *to squeeze into shape and mold into form, especially as a potter*. God is the Potter and He knows how He formed us; He knows that we were made of dust. This is why God has compassion on us.

But, why would God use this substance to make man? It seems a very purposeful move. The Bible chooses its words carefully. Apparently, God wanted us to be aware of the fact that the animals and plant life were made of the *ground* while man was made of the *dust* of the ground.

```
Hell Dust; it was what he was made of
```

Imagine what that dust contained. This dust was produced when the most hideous of creatures was propelled from the presence of God thus colliding with a hell from beneath that was quaking violently in anticipation of his coming! The dust, of which Adam was formed, was tainted with the very rebellion of Satan. That explains all of the negative Biblical connotations concerning dust. It also explains Adam's lustful, rebellious disposition. Although Elohim created man perfectly, Jehovah Elohim formed man of Hell dust.

God, Elohim, did indeed create Adam perfectly in His image, but the material Jehovah Elohim used to form him bent Adam toward evil, *"The creature was made subject to vanity, not willingly, but by reason of Him Who subjected the same in hope..."*

This explains how man could be created perfectly by God and also formed hell bent by the LORD God. Elohim *created* mankind good and then Jehovah Elohim *formed* that very mankind out of bad stuff.

This had everything to do with God and nothing to do with man, *"Nay but, O man, who art thou that repliest against God? Shall the thing formed say to him that formed it, Why hast thou made me thus?"* God owns all power and with this power He chose to make man out of hell dust. Shall we, the thing formed, say to Him that formed us, "Why have you made me this way?"

Now we are beginning to see a master plan. Jehovah Elohim purposely formed Adam from evil dust so that he had no choice but to sin. We saw this sin nature manifest in the Garden of Eden.

Jehovah Elohim formed Adam from hell dust (which gave him this sin nature) and then He gave him a commandment to bristle that sin nature to the surface, *"And the LORD God commanded the man, saying, Of every tree of the garden thou mayest freely eat: But of the tree of the knowledge of good and evil, thou shalt not eat of it: for in the day that thou eatest thereof thou shalt surely die." (For without the law sin was dead),* and then He allowed the serpent to entice His hell bent man, *"Now the serpent was more subtle than any beast of the field which the LORD God had made. And he said unto the woman..."* and the result was sin and death, *"For sin, taking occasion by the commandment, deceived me, and by it slew me."*

God came to hell/earth, brought in His light and Truth, divided the two, and then formed man in such a way as to be bent toward the lies and the darkness so that He could woo them to the Truth by delivering them from the bondage of corruption and making them His sons. Mission accomplished.

Free to be Holy

> "And they were both naked, the man and his wife, and were not ashamed."
> **Genesis 2:25**

Beyond Eden

I never ceased to be amazed by how much important information is crammed into the creation and fall of man as it is recorded in the first three chapters of Genesis. Now that we understand how Adam was predestined to sin from the moment of his formation, we are better able to understand what it was really like in the Garden of Eden.

No Garden walk

Undoubtedly, the Garden of Eden was a beautiful place with a wonderful atmosphere of peace, joy, and serenity. The weather was probably pristine and the vistas breathtaking. Biblically, we know that the Tree of Life is in heaven (Rev 22), and we know the Tree of Life was in the Garden of Eden (Gen 2:9). That tells us that the Garden of Eden was a heavenly place. So, praise God, mankind is certainly destined to end up back in this Edenic atmosphere.

However, what mankind is *not* destined to go back to is the particular type of relationship that God shared with Adam and Eve before they sinned. Neither is man destined to go back to Adam and Eve's pre-sin disposition. Although it is a commonly taught precept, Christianity *does not* recreate in us the relationship that God shared with Adam and Eve before they sinned. There are too many differences between the two to make this assertion. Let's explore the relationship Adam and Eve shared with God before they sinned. I think you will find that it was not all that it's cracked up to be.

In the Garden of Eden, there was separation

I am a bit disturbed by the relationship Adam and Eve seemed to share with God. There is no indication of any kind of fondness in their relationship. We have heard it said that they walked together in the cool of the day, but that is a misconception.

The Bible never says that God walked *together* with Adam and Eve. We know that Adam and Eve, *"heard the voice of the LORD God walking in the garden in the cool of the day"*, but that tells us next to nothing. We must not leap to the conclusion that they walked *together* in the cool of the day just because God was walking in the garden in the cool of the day while Adam was threading a needle and Eve was cutting a pattern from a leaf.

We have an entire chapter in Hebrews dedicated to giving us a list of Bible heroes and describing the sort of relationship they had with God. Adam and Eve are not in this list. We cannot assume Adam and Eve were left out because they sinned, as all of those who are featured in that chapter sinned. If what Adam and Eve shared with God was so exceptional that destiny would dictate that it would be *our* ultimate end, we should know more about it.

The only emotional picture we get concerning Adam is that God thought it not good that he be alone. We don't know how Adam felt about being alone. We really don't know anything at all about Adam. God formed the animals and the birds and brought them to Adam so that he could name them. We do not get even a morsel of information about how that went.

Not finding a suitable mate, from one of Adam's ribs God made Eve. Finally Adam speaks and simply makes a declaration concerning what had happened. From that point all we get is the episode with the serpent. We have no love stories concerning Adam's amazing, miraculous new wife, no, not one word of commentary.

Adam was used as a vessel for four extremely important tasks: Being the very first human, working the very first garden, naming the original animal kingdom, and being the very first husband. Are there no stories to go with these amazing events?

How disturbing that Adam and Eve were not with God at the time of their temptation. These two were alone when they got to the tree, and alone when they were tempted by the serpent, and alone when they ate of the fruit, and alone when they discovered their nakedness. That is a lot of alone time for two creatures that were supposedly living the ultimate "God" life.

We are privileged to watch Moses and Abraham become friends of

God, God speaks of David as a man after His own heart, and we watched Elijah get ministered to by angels before he hears the "still, small voice" of God. There are many other examples, just like these, concerning those who shared intimacy with God. The Bible loves to tell noteworthy stories. However, when we look at the story of Adam and Eve, we get no images of trust, love, or even companionship; just rote facts.

More quandaries:
Too easy to sin & too easy to hide

I am also troubled by the fact that Adam and Eve did not seem alarmed by a being that was defying their beloved Lord. Where was their passion for God? These two didn't even put up a fight! Eve gave in to the thirty-second temptation of the serpent, but apparently Adam didn't even need that much prompting. After conversing with the serpent and quickly giving in, Eve ate of the fruit and, *"gave also unto her husband with her; and he did eat."* That's it…end of story.

Adam apparently didn't even argue with his wife. Think about that. God had given this guy just one command! Adam could do anything he wanted except eat of that tree and he was warned that he would die if he did eat of it.

If Adam was living this great life of ultimate intimacy with God, then why when Eve offered him a bite of forbidden fruit did he just open his mouth and take it without hesitation? Something doesn't add up.

It also puzzles me that Adam and Eve could *hide* from God, the all-knowing One, to the point that God was prompted to ask, *"Where art thou?"* To further this, God went on to ask Adam who had told him he was naked and then He asked if they had eaten of the tree. That's a lot of questions for an omnipresent God!

Where was God?

Does this relationship seem a little detached to you? It doesn't necessarily seem like a *bad* relationship, but was it ideal? I mean, where was God when Adam and Eve were meeting the serpent, apparently unaware of his deceptive means? Did God really leave His only two humans alone to face this one who comes only to steal, kill, and destroy?

Up to the moment they partook of their evil meal, Adam and Eve had only known Truth. In order to prepare Adam and Eve for the serpent's lies, it would have been necessary for God to school them concerning good and evil just as we have been schooled in preparation for the enemy, *"Put on the whole armour of God, that ye may be able to stand against the wiles of the devil...Be sober, be vigilant; because your adversary the devil, as a roaring lion, walketh about, seeking whom he may devour:" (Eph 6:11 & 1Pet 5:8 KJV)*. However, we learn from the naming of the forbidden tree that all knowledge of good and evil was locked into the very fruit they had been commanded not to eat.

The concept of evil had never even entered the minds of our newly formed couple. We must consider the idea that God allowed the serpent access to a very ignorant and vulnerable Adam and Eve. These two walked into Satan's trap with their eyes wide shut. Adam and Eve had no reason to believe that a being could be lying to them; they didn't even understand the concept of a lie!

This may explain Adam and Eve's apathetic response to the temptation of the serpent, "Really? We won't die? We'll be wise like God? Cool." How could they know he was lying? How could they really know anything? Separate the knowledge of good and evil from your mind, if you can, and try to think one coherent thought. It is impossible to be an emotional, or even a rational being without the conceptual idea of evil.

Ill equipped

So, one would think that if Adam and Eve were ill equipped to battle against their one enemy, God wouldn't have let them out of His sight, *"There hath no temptation taken you but such as is common to man: but God is faithful, who will not suffer you to be tempted above that ye are able; but will with the temptation also make a way to escape, that ye may be able to bear it." (1 Cor 10:13 KJV).*

Our New Testament verse makes it sound like God is ever present with those who are being tempted, helping them and showing them a way of escape. If what we have through Christ mimics the Edenic experience, then where was God when Adam and Eve were being tempted? Was He faithful to show them a way of escape? If He had been, He wouldn't have entered stage left *after the fact* and asked Adam where he was. God knew of the impending showdown; He is not ignorant of anything. But there they were, alone and ill equipped.

Nakedness

The other thing that bothers me about Adam and Eve is that they were naked. The Bible, when speaking of the Father, the Son, the angels, and the departed saints, depicts them in clothing.

When speaking of God, Isaiah says, *"...I saw also the Lord sitting upon a throne, high and lifted up, and his train filled the temple." (Isa 6:1 KJV).* According to the Hebrew definition, God's train is His skirt. Likewise, Jesus has clothing, *"And in the midst of the seven candlesticks one like unto the Son of man, clothed with a garment down to the foot, and girt about the paps with a golden girdle." (Rev 1:13 KJV).* Neither of these describes nakedness of any kind. Adam and Eve were described as naked.

As well, we know that the angels are clothed because angels are commonly mistaken as men in the Bible and Paul instructs us, *"Be not forgetful to entertain strangers: for thereby some have entertained angels unawares." (Heb 13:2 KJV)*. And, finally, we know that the saints in heaven are clothed, *"After this I beheld, and, lo, a great multitude, which no man could number, of all nations, and kindreds, and people, and tongues, stood before the throne, and before the Lamb, clothed with white robes, and palms in their hands;" (Rev 7:9 KJV)*. It seems that everyone from God on down is wearing some sort of clothing. So why were Adam and Eve described as naked?

I find it very interesting that though our information about Adam and Eve is sparse, we are given this tiny piece of information concerning their emotional state before the fall, *"And they were both naked, the man and his wife, and were not ashamed."*

Feathers and fur

Surely all clothing was not "invented" as a result of Adam and Eve's sin. Did God have to don a robe because Adam and Eve sinned? That is ridiculous. Some have said that Adam and Eve were clothed with spiritual clothing that grew from the inside out much like feathers on a bird or fur on an animal. However, no one calls a feathered bird or a furry animal naked. These are only naked when they are missing feathers and fur. God would not have called Adam and Eve naked if they had natural clothing.

I'm sure God's clothing is spiritually induced; yet He is never referred to as naked. Jesus had on natural clothing when He walked on earth, now He has heavenly clothing. Jesus was not and is not naked. The Bible would not refer to Adam and Eve as "naked" if they were clothed as God, Jesus, the angels, and the saints are clothed. If Adam and Eve were referred to as naked it is because they were!

We are given sparse information about Adam and Eve; but what we have been told is that first they were naked and unashamed, and then they sinned and felt shame. Genesis says that immediately after they ate of the fruit they *knew* they were naked. It does not say that when they ate the fruit they *became* naked. Adam and Eve were naked in every sense of the word but they did not *know* it until they ate that fruit.

Taking crafty counsel

The Hebrew root word for "naked" is "aram" and means, *to be (or make) bare...to be cunning (usually in a bad sense)...beware, take crafty [counsel], be prudent, deal subtly.* This definition includes both a physical and spiritual nakedness. One of the spiritual attributes is "taking crafty counsel". Isn't that exactly what Adam and Eve did immediately before they recognized they were naked? When their spiritual nakedness manifested, Adam and Eve noticed their physical nakedness.

Adam and Eve were naked and unashamed before they ate that fruit because they were unaware of their wretched hell bent state and therefore had not yet received their salvation garments to cover their wretched hell bent state. Adam and Eve had not yet been "clothed from on high" because they didn't know they needed to be!

A pristine life?

What have we learned about Adam and his pristine life in the Garden of Eden?

1. His life was not noteworthy.
2. He was not always in the presence of God.
3. He was easily tempted.
4. He was ill equipped for the wiles of the devil.
5. He was naked.

What we read of the born-again believer's relationship with God in the Gospel of John is in sharp contrast to this description. While praying for His disciples and those to whom the Gospel would eventually reach, Jesus said this:

> "And I will pray the Father, and he shall give you another Comforter, **that he may abide with you for ever;** (that would have been handy for Adam and Eve when they faced the serpent...) Even the **Spirit of truth;** (again, handy) whom the world cannot receive, because it seeth him not, neither knoweth him: but ye know him; for **he dwelleth with you**, and shall be in you. I will not leave you comfortless: I will come to you. Yet a little while, and the world seeth me no more; but ye see me: because I live, ye shall live also. At that day ye shall know that
> **I am in my Father, and ye in me, and I in you."**
> (John 14:16-20 KJV emphasis and parenthesis mine).

Jesus emphatically states that He is *in* His Father and we are *in* Him and He is *in* us; united together permanently. So Jesus affords the New Testament believer this kind of communion while Adam and Eve were left clueless, powerless, and alone to look down the barrel of a gun.

What's wrong with this picture?

According to the New Testament, the death and resurrection of Christ affords us the honor to, *"...be filled with the knowledge of his will in all wisdom and spiritual understanding; That ye might walk worthy of the Lord unto all pleasing, being fruitful in every good work, and increasing in the knowledge of God; Strengthened with all might, according to his glorious power, unto all patience and longsuffering with joyfulness;" (Col 1:9-11 KJV).*

Does this description fit Adam before he sinned? Was Adam filled with the knowledge of God's will in all wisdom and spiritual understanding? Was Adam walking worthy of the Lord, pleasing Him in all he did, being fruitful in every good work and increasing in knowledge? Was Adam strengthened with all might according to God's glorious power, unto all patience and longsuffering with joyfulness?

If Adam had wisdom and spiritual understanding, he would have at least put up more of a fight. If Adam had been strengthened with all might according to God's glorious power, he would have possessed the strength to stand up to the temptation. If Adam had been walking worthy of the Lord, pleasing Him in all he did, and being fruitful in every good work, he would not have disobeyed.

It was different then

You may argue, "Hey, as Christians we have all these things and we still sin!" That is true, but things are a bit different now. We are living on the *cursed* side of the flaming sword. Although not an excuse, the curse certainly offers an explanation for our behavior.

All capacity for sin has been opened up to us and we are living in a cursed world. We are battered, beaten, and abused by this world every day that we live in it. All of our excuses for sin are in place; we are hungry, so we steal, hurt, so we take revenge, and angry, so we dishonor. Unlike Adam, we, as Christians, do not just blithely sin away without giving it a second thought.

Adam and Eve did not have these negative experiences. They were not battered, beaten, and abused. They were not hungry. They were not hurt. They had no reason to be angry. There was no logical reason for them to sin if they had both the Edenic environment *and* what has been offered to us through the sacrifice of Christ. Adam and Eve were over there, before sin had even been introduced and while their environment was yet perfect!

What was their excuse? Why did they sin?

I can't even imagine what it would be like to be created by God, placed in perfect surroundings, my every need met, in the physical presence of God, and having in my possession all the promises of the New Testament. Again, if the work of the cross brings us back to Eden, that means that everything promised in the New Testament was in manifestation in Eden. If Adam, living in the protection and blessing of Eden, had what has been offered to us through Christ, he had a fail-safe situation. There was no logical reason for him to sin.

From this New Testament verse, and many others like it, we can only conclude that Adam was *not* operating in the same power that is offered to the born-again Christian. What that tells us is that the two are not the same. If the work of the cross brings us back to pre-sin Adam, then pre-sin Adam should look and operate like a successful born-again Christian. However, he does not; he doesn't even come close. New Testament Christianity goes way beyond Eden.

Here we go again?

What hope do we, who are born-again, have against the power of temptation if all we are afforded is the Edenic experience? After all, Adam and Eve *did* sin. They *did* fall for the temptation of the serpent. In the book of Luke, Jesus makes a key statement, *"And he said unto them, I beheld Satan as lightning fall from heaven. Behold, I give unto you power to tread on serpents and scorpions, and over all the power of the enemy: and nothing shall by any means hurt you." (10:18-19 KJV)*.

If Adam and Eve had power to tread on serpents and scorpions and power over all the power of the enemy, they would not have succumbed to the serpent's temptation. But they *did* yield to this temptation, which means that they were not walking in this power.

So what if it is true? What if the work of Jesus *does* take us back to the Garden of Eden? Won't the same thing happen again? If what we get through Christ does not go beyond Eden, then neither will it afford us the ability to *behave* beyond Eden.

If Adam sinned even while endued with "Christian" power, then I fear that I, under the provision of the cross, will be equally susceptible to sin. What will be the difference between Adam and me? Where is the power to tread on serpents?

Going further, I must ask, what will keep this behavior from following us into heaven? Tell me, what is the difference? What has changed? Why will we not sin in heaven if we do not have any more power than Adam had?

You may think, well, Satan will no longer be there to tempt us. It is true that he will not be there, but, I hardly think the only reason we won't sin in heaven is because there will be no devil to tempt us. That doesn't seem genuine. What good is it if a man only stays true to his wife when other women aren't around? That type of loyalty has no value.

If empty, forced obedience was all God was after He wouldn't have given Satan access to the garden to begin with. And, yes, I believe the devil had full access to the Garden of Eden. There is no scriptural indication that Satan had the power to tread where he wasn't allowed, thus interrupting God's predestined path for all of mankind. When a doctrine doesn't add up with the Bible's description of God, we must reevaluate the doctrine.

You see, none of our preconceived notions about Genesis make sense. Adam and Eve did not have victory over sin. In Christ, we are promised victory over the devil right in his face, not as a result of his absence. That is what the cross provides. Adam and Eve did not have that victory.

He was no Moses

So, we can see that what Adam and Eve experienced in the Garden of Eden was not ideal. This Genesis account stands out as the only significant Biblical story lacking passion. We don't know anything about Adam. We don't know what kind of relationship he had with God, or if he even had a close, personal relationship with Him. We are told that Adam named the birds and the animals and God walked in the garden in the cool of the day. That is all.

If the life Adam experienced before he sinned was perfect and if his pre-sin life is our consummate end, shouldn't we know more about that life? Shouldn't we know more about pre-sin Adam? When it comes to other key figures in the Bible, we know a generous amount. We usually know things we wish we didn't know.

Abraham was faithful, Noah was righteous, Moses was a great leader, David was a warrior, Isaiah was passionate, Elijah was powerful, and Solomon was wise. Abraham was also a liar and an adulterer, Noah was a drunkard, Moses was a coward and a murderer, David was an adulterer and a murderer, Isaiah was a man of unclean lips, Elijah was a man of like passions, and what shall we say of Solomon who depressed us with his ecclesiastical account of his unsuccessful pursuit of happiness?

But what was Adam? We don't know anything good or bad about him. All we know about him was that he named the animals and then he sinned. This nondescript life is to what we are supposed to return?

All we see when we look into the Garden of Eden is a man named Adam who seemed to be set on a course for hell. Adam was ignorant of the devices of evil, given the capacity to sin, a commandment to empower that sin, and then left alone with the father of all lies. This does not sound like the kind of situation I would like to go back to.

From a different view

I once learned that words account for only seven percent of communication while the other ninety-three percent is made up of inflection and tone. Therefore, the written word is void of inflection and tone. A story can have a very different meaning when its tone and inflection are changed. There are many movies that depict the life of Christ. In most of these, He seems a very sober person who speaks in a low tone with a British accent. I don't see Him this way. I believe Jesus was quite animated and probably spoke in the dialect of His people.

If I were with you in person, I would be able to demonstrate to you, by the inflections and tones in my voice, how I believe Jesus communicated. But, this is the written word, so I cannot, which is my point. The Bible is a *written* account of words that were spoken. We are left to introduce our own inflections and tones to the written words. Our understanding of the Scriptures will influence these inflections, right, wrong, or otherwise. We picture an angry God in Genesis because we deem the fall of man a catastrophic event.

Do we really believe this?

Just yesterday, I actually heard a nationally respected preacher say that after Adam and Eve sinned, God had to figure out a way to fix the situation. This preacher of the Gospel went on to say that had God tried to fix the problem on the spot without being a man, it would have been an "illegal" move and Satan would have been able to "put God's lights out". You're kidding me. The moment the God of all Truth makes a move it can no longer be called "illegal". And as far as "putting God's lights out", there is not enough paper in the world to do justice to the absurdity of this statement.

Can you just picture God sitting on a rock in the garden with His elbow on His knee, chin cupped in His hand, and a furrowed brow, "This is a pickle I tell you…a real pickle. Boy I didn't see that coming. Where does Lucifer get off coming into My garden after I condemned him to Hell? Well, it just goes to show you, you can't trust anyone. Note to self: Keep sharp eye on devil. Jesus, come here. Do you have anything planned for the next seven thousand years? Good…gonna need you. It's a wild plan, but I have myself a situation like you wouldn't believe. I turn my back for five minutes and Lucifer snakes his way in the back door of the garden and the next thing I know my two created beings are taking sewing classes. One wrong move from Me at this point and it will all be over for Us and man!"

We must not insult our God in this way. I do not believe for one minute that the All Powerful God was ever cornered by surprise. Let us please remember Who He is.

A different spin

I don't believe God was in a rage when He found out that Adam and Eve had eaten the fruit. As I have said before, I think He full well expected it. Jehovah Elohim made man from hell dust which gave him a nature that longed for things forbidden, then He forbad him to eat a particular fruit, and finally, He left him alone in the garden with the serpent: Satan incarnate. It doesn't take a rocket scientist to figure out what is eventually going to happen.

So, let's try something just for fun. Let's change God's inflection and tone in Genesis and see what happens. I am going to play a bit loose with the wording, but will not change its meaning. We have always pictured God flying into a rage of indignation as He cursed Adam, Eve, and the Serpent. This time, let's picture a God Who knew this was going to happen and simply responded the way He had predetermined to respond. After all, the Lamb *was* slain from the foundations of the world.

So we'll take away the angry face and replace it with an understanding face, take away the surprised tone and replace it with a controlled tone, and take away the rage and replace it with a glint of anticipation in the eyes of God, (His plan is finally going to get off the ground):

The Lord God called out to Adam, *"Where are you?"*

Adam responds, *"I heard you coming and I was afraid because I am naked, so I hid myself."*

With a nod of His head, God asks, *"Who told you that you were naked? Have you eaten the fruit that I told you not to eat?"*

And the man answered, *"The woman that You gave me offered me the fruit and I ate it."*

The Lord turns His gaze toward Eve and simply asked her, *"What have you done?"*

And the woman said, *"The serpent enticed me and I fell to his temptation and ate."*

How about that? It all happened just as God planned. Now we are in the second phase of the plan.

So the Lord turns His attention to the serpent and begins to lay out his foreordained future plans, *"Because you have done this, you will be cursed above all cattle and every beast of the field. Down on your belly you will go, prostrate to Me forever. You will eat your own dust all the days of your life. And there will be hatred between you and the woman and between your child and her child. He shall bruise your head while you merely bruise His heel."*

And then God turned to the woman and, again, laid out His foreordained plans for her, *"This is how it will be for you: I will greatly multiply your sorrow at conception and in sorrow will you bring forth your children. Your desire shall be to your husband, but he will rule over you."*

Now it was Adam's turn, *"Because you listened to your wife and ate of the tree which I commanded you not to eat, the ground is now cursed for your sake. You will labor to eat of it all the days of your life. It will bring forth thorns and thistles, but you will still have to eat of it. You will sweat for your bread until you return to the ground from which you were taken. For you are made of dust and you will return to dust."*

Delivered from corruption

God has just described the very corruption to which He had planned to deliver us as per Romans 8:20-21, *"For the creature was made subject to vanity, not willingly, but by reason of him who hath subjected the same in hope, Because the creature itself also shall be **delivered from the bondage of corruption** into the glorious liberty of the children of God."*

God made it so that the woman would be constantly frustrated by her desire for her husband and the man would be constantly frustrated by his work. God hit the male and female right where they lived.

A woman finds her identity in her man and a man finds his identity in his work. Women always want more out of men and men always want more out of work. The curse set up mankind to be in constant need of deliverance, *"Because the creature itself also shall be delivered from the bondage of corruption into the glorious liberty of the children of God."*

Following this, Adam named his wife Eve and then God proceeded to make clothes for them. You see, Adam and Eve responded to their nakedness in exactly the same way that all humans respond to their spiritual nakedness; they tried to cover themselves with something they created themselves. This fleshly covering is never more than awkward and fleeting.

God showed Adam and Eve that their attempts to cover their nakedness were insufficient and that is why, *"Unto Adam also and to his wife did the LORD God make coats of skins, and clothed them." (Gen 3:21 KJV).* Adam and Eve needed more than physical clothing. Their leaves only covered the outward manifestation of an inward nakedness

In order to make coats of skins, animals were sacrificed. This was the very first animal sacrifice that was used to symbolize the sacrifice of the Lamb of God. From this point, Adam and Eve were no longer spiritually naked; they were symbolically clothed with Christ in the very same way that all Old Testament believers were clothed with Christ through symbolic animal sacrifice.

The Genesis

Now we can see why we don't go back to Adam's hell bent state nor do we go back to the non-descript relationship he had with God. There are better things in store; things that God had planned all along. You see there is a reason why the first book of the Bible is called "Genesis"; it was the *beginning* of the experience of mankind on the earth. All the rest was planned but had not yet come to pass.

Our story in Genesis does not tell us to what we must return, it simply tells us how things began. Throughout the Bible we see many more things happen. All that happened had purpose and timing just as the life and sin of Adam had purpose and timing. Adam was the beginning, or Genesis, of creation. In addition to this, we also have a middle, and we have an end. These are chronicled in the same Bible that tells the story of the beginning.

When we look back over Biblical history, we see a very definite progression of mankind from the garden to Jesus:

1. Our natural father, Adam, had sin although no relationship.
2. Our spiritual father, Abraham, had sin and a relationship.
3. The children of Israel who were *"ensamples"* for us, had a relationship and a covering for their sin through the Levitical Priesthood.
4. Jesus had a relationship and power over sin.
5. We are alive in Christ and share in His inheritance: Relationship and power over sin.

> *"O death, where is thy sting? O grave, where is thy victory? The sting of death is sin; and the strength of sin is the law. But thanks be to God, which giveth us the victory through our Lord Jesus Christ."*
> *1 Cor 15:55-57 KJV)*

What a view!

In these last days we have a unique vantage point. Because we are living in the last days, we can see the whole picture simply by looking backward! We see the beginning in Genesis, the middle through the Law and the Prophets, and the end in the New Testament. We look at the Bible and see the flow along the time line.

The Bible says there is a season for everything. There was a season to create a man who would need a Savior, a season to point that man in the direction of the coming Savior, a season to manifest the Savior, and a season for mankind to walk in that salvation.

The Beginning

Before Adam sinned, we are given no more than a remote view of God. We see what He does, the power He has, and the authority

He possesses, but not much else. From the information we have been given, we have no indication that there existed any closeness between God and His created man. God was on a mission to get this ball rolling and that is what He did. This was the beginning.

The Middle

After Adam sinned and up until the time that Jesus came, we see just the opposite. We see a very relational God Who is extremely emotional. Consider how God fluctuated in His emotions and His modes during this middle time: He made man, and then He cursed man, then He repented that He made man. He flooded the earth, and then made a promise to never do that again.

God then goes on to heroically deliver His people from Egypt only to go into a rage on Mount Sinai and ask Moses to move out of His way so that He could destroy them and start over. All through the prophets we hear Him wail as a Lover torn between deliverance and wrath as His relationship with His people goes through the ups and downs of a very real love affair. This was the middle.

The End

And, finally, in these end times we are given the last will and testament of God through the Gospel of Jesus Christ. God is now Scripturally silent. There is no more to write. It is finished. The picture with which God left us is one of peace and rest. During this dispensation, we see Jesus sitting at the right hand of the Father, waiting till His enemies be made His footstool (He 10:13). We have been invited to join Him. This is the end. All is finished and just waiting to be manifested in His bride.

It is finished

The events that began in the Garden of Eden are now summed up in these last days. When Jesus appeared to John in Revelation, He said, *"I am Alpha and Omega, the beginning and the ending"* (Rev

1:8). God started something and He has brought it to an end. God's will is at last accomplished through the completed work of Christ, which, by the way, goes *way* beyond Eden.

Free to be Holy

> "Moreover the law entered, that the offence might abound. But where sin abounded, grace did much more abound: That as sin hath reigned unto death, even so might grace reign through righteousness unto eternal life by Jesus Christ our Lord."
> **Romans 5:20 - 21**

A Seed Sown

God has purpose in all of His doings. We are going to explore many of these. Right now we are going to consider one of the reasons God created Adam to die. Although I do not believe in the theory of the *physical* evolution of man, I do believe very much in the *spiritual* evolution of mankind.

Free to be Holy

According to the Encarta World English Dictionary, the biology developmental process of evolution is this: *The natural or artificially induced process by which new and different organisms develop as a result of changes in genetic material.* Well, born-again Christians are new and different creatures due to a change in genetic material. We are going to go into this in depth in a later chapter, but for now we are going to look at how this process was initiated in the creation of mankind.

Adam was a beautiful creature as he was made in the image of God, but he was a far cry from the vision God had for mankind. However, mankind evolved into *"the glorious liberty of the sons of God"* through the cycle of life and death much the same way that a caterpillar evolves into a butterfly through a sort of "death" (after all, once we have the butterfly, the caterpillar is no more).

We have already discussed how we learn about the spiritual realm by studying the natural. *"For the invisible things of him from the creation of the world are clearly seen, being understood by the things that are made..." (Rom 1:20 KJV).* All around us are pictures and examples of those things that we cannot see with our eyes. God uses these natural counterparts to the spiritual realm as object lessons that help us to understand Him and the way He functions within His spiritual realm.

A picture is worth a thousand words

Our verse from above specifically tells us that there are invisible things of God from the creation of the world that are understood through natural examples. Paul reminds us of this concept when he speaks of marriage in the book of Ephesians. He speaks of how a wife should submit to her husband, as he is her "head", and how a husband should love his wife even as Christ loves the church.

Paul sums up this teaching concerning marriage by saying this, *"This is a great mystery: but I speak concerning Christ and the church." (Eph 5:32 KJV).* Paul is reminding this church that our experiences on earth are types, pictures, and examples of preeminent Truths in the spiritual realm. The primary purpose of the functions of this life is to teach us the functions of the spiritual realm.

```
Sowing and reaping
```

As well, the laws of sowing and reaping are primarily spiritual. The physical example of this spiritual Truth exists to teach us a lesson about God and His spiritual realm. As a matter of fact, Jesus went so far as to use the physical example of sowing and reaping to illustrate the very kingdom of God:

> *"...So is the kingdom of God, as if a man should cast seed into the ground; And should sleep, and rise night and day, and the seed should spring and grow up, he knoweth not how. For the earth bringeth forth fruit of herself; first the blade, then the ear, after that the full corn in the ear. But when the fruit is brought forth, immediately he putteth in the sickle, because the harvest is come."*
> *(Mark 4:26-29 KJV)*

When did the kingdom of God begin? Hasn't the kingdom of God always existed? Of courses it has. So when Jesus speaks of how the kingdom of God works, He is speaking concerning God and how He has always worked. We must take this lesson about the kingdom of God all the way back to Genesis. When God created the heavens and the earth He was sowing seeds.

Jesus said that we understand the kingdom of God by studying the workings of seeds that are sown in the earth. The entire kingdom of God functions as a seed sown. A very small seed is buried, and a plant issues forth which is in accordance with whatever was planted.

The Seed

If the kingdom of God is as a seed that has been planted, then we must take some time to study this phenomenon. Jesus gives us a head start by explaining how it is a miracle of sorts in that after it is sown, all we have to do is wait and eventually the seed will become a plant. But we must move back a step. One cannot just plant any seed. There is one particular kind of seed that will never become a plant--even when it is sown: A live seed.

A Seed must die

One cannot pluck an ear of corn off of a live plant, remove a kernel, and sow it directly into the earth and expect a harvest. That kernel of corn must die before it can be sown, *"...what you sow is not made alive unless it dies." (1 Cor 15:36 NKJV)*.

However, the entire seed does not die; only the outer shell must die. A natural seed is bi-part; it is comprised of an outer shell and an inner root. When the outer shell dies, it is then sown and decomposes quickly to expose the inner root to the soil where it can be fed. As the root extracts water and nutrients from the soil, it begins to grow.

If the kingdom of God *is as a seed when it is sown in the earth*, then, as well, seeds that are sown in the kingdom of God must die before they can be sown. Paul illustrates this to the church in Corinth when speaking of the resurrection of life, *"So also is the resurrection of the dead. It is sown in corruption; it is raised in incorruption:" (1 Cor 15:42 KJV)*.

Our very transition from earth to Heaven will involve corruption and death before we will experience incorruption and eternal life. The word "corruption" means decay and ruin. Before a seed can be planted it must die. After the seed is dead it must be sown in this state of decay and ruin before it can be raised in incorruption.

The least of all seeds

Jesus goes on to give us more information about the kingdom of God. Again, He uses the example of a seed:

> *"And he said, Whereunto shall we liken the kingdom of God? or with what comparison shall we compare it? It is like a grain of mustard seed, which, when it is sown in the earth, is less than all the seeds that be in the earth: But when it is sown, it groweth up, and becometh greater than all herbs, and shooteth out great branches; so that the fowls of the air may lodge under the shadow of it."*
> *(Mark 4:30-32 KJV)*

In particular, the kingdom of God is not just as a seed that is sown in the earth; it is compared to the mustard seed, which Jesus said is less than all the other seeds. However, when it grows up it becomes greater than the rest. So not only is the kingdom of God compared to a seed, but the *least* of all seeds with the potential to be the greatest of all.

If we go back to our Scriptures from First Corinthians, we see that Paul further comments on the type of seed that brings forth a good harvest, *"It is sown in dishonour; it is raised in glory: it is sown in weakness; it is raised in power:"* (1 Cor 15:43 KJV). So we see that a seed is very different from the plant that issues from it. A seed is dead, small, dishonorable, and weak whereas a plant is alive, large, flourishing, and strong.

The Sower sows the Word

In the parable of the sower, Jesus compares the seed with the Word of God and the soil with the human heart, *"When any one heareth the word of the kingdom, and understandeth it not, then cometh the wicked one, and catcheth away that which was sown in his heart.*

This is he which received seed by the way side." (Matt 13:19 KJV).

Earlier, Jesus taught His disciples that the kingdom of God is as a seed sown in the earth. Now, while telling the <u>parable of the sower</u>, Jesus says that if we don't understand how the kingdom of God works, the enemy will steal the Word sown. So we are behooved to understand that the kingdom of God, from everlasting to everlasting, is *as a seed sown*.

God sows His Word into the hearts of men. God sowed seeds in the Garden of Eden that needed water and a man to bring forth a harvest. Jesus describes God's very kingdom as a seed when it is sown. Finally, we know that God employs the laws of sowing and reaping in His creative process. God is a Gardener like no other.

Adam

Now that we understand the physics of a seed, the process of sowing, and the fact that God uses this practice, we must take another look at Adam. After all, the invisible things of God are understood by things that are made.

When God made Adam, He formed him from hell dust and then blew life into his nostrils, *"And the LORD God formed man of the dust of the ground, and breathed into his nostrils the breath of life; and man became a living soul." (Gen 2:7 KJV).* By this definition, Adam became a seed; he had a worthless outer shell that had to go and a lively inner root that had to grow.

Now that Adam is a seed, can God plant him? No; he is still alive, *"That which thou sowest is not made alive unless it dies."* Adam had to die before God could plant him. In order to produce this death, the law had to be brought into the picture because, *"The sting of death is sin; and the strength of sin is the law." (1 Cor 15:56 KJV).*

When Adam ate that fruit he experienced immediate spiritual death. That spiritual death brought a physical death. When that physical death came, Adam was buried in the earth as a natural example of a spiritual Truth. Adam died spiritually and physically, and he was sown spiritually and physically.

Have seed; need garden plot

I now find it fascinating that God placed Adam in a garden. Just picture it: God puts man under the authority of the sin nature by forming him of hell dust, He breathes into his nostrils the breath of His life thus making him a seed, and then He gives this man a law knowing that *"when the law entered, sin would revive, and he would die."*, and finally, *"And the LORD God planted a garden eastward in Eden; and there he put the man whom he had formed."* (Gen 2:8 KJV).

Doesn't this seem like an early spring day in the garden? I can picture God dressed in overalls and gloves with a hoe in his hand and a smile on His face just waiting for His seed to die so He could plant him.

Far greater

When God sows a seed, it is for the purpose of bringing forth something that is far greater than the seed. So what could be greater than a man made in the image of God? A Son made in the image of God Who would bring many more sons unto glory! A seed is dead, small, and singular whereas the plant that issues forth is alive, growing, and multiplying.

Adam, being completely hell bent, was the "least of all seeds", but when he was sown that harvest brought the Messiah Who was greater than all. Jesus shot out great branches. Adam died in dishonor and weakness; Jesus was raised in glory. Jesus died a man despised and we were raised in the power of His resurrection.

One small seed produces a huge tree bearing much fruit. When Jehovah Elohim sowed Adam, He reaped a tremendous harvest. Just as a grain of mustard seed, when Adam was sown he was the least of all seeds and when the harvest came, not only was it of excellent value, it was packed with produce.

Harvest of Son and sons

God had a great plan in mind, but it wasn't being pals with a created being; He had angels for that. God's plan was to have offspring. We know that He was pleased with His Son, Jesus, but God was not finished, *"For **it became him**, for whom are all things, and by whom are all things, **in bringing many sons unto glory**..." (Heb 2:10 KJV emphasis mine)*. To say "it became Him" in bring many sons to glory, is to say that it was fitting and proper for God to bring *many sons* unto glory.

Son

For God, having a Son was the most natural thing to do! God planned and intended to bring forth His Son from the foundation of the world, *"Who verily was foreordained before the foundation of the world, but was manifest in these last times for you," (1 Pet 1:20 KJV)*. When Jesus finally came, God predictably said, *"This is my beloved Son in Whom I am well pleased."* God was well pleased with Jesus because a Son was what He desired in the first place; God simply used the cycle of life and death to produce a Son because HE IS A SOWER and the kingdom of God is AS A SEED SOWN.

sons

Although God was very pleased with His Son, He was not finished. God's great plan was to bring many *sons* unto glory, *"For it became him, for whom are all things, and by whom are all things, in bringing many **sons** unto glory..."* As well, we remember from our verse in Romans that God subjected us to vanity because He had hope to deliver us from this bondage of corruption into the glorious liberty of the *children* of God. Now we are about to see how this plan went from God's desire to our destiny:

> *"According as he hath chosen us in him before the foundation of the world...Having predestinated us unto the adoption of **children** by Jesus Christ to himself, according to the good pleasure of his will,"* (Eph 1:4a&5 KJV emphasis mine).

Adam was no son

Adam was a creation, however, God wanted a Son. A child is not made; a child is born. So in saying that God wanted sons, the Bible is saying that God wanted to give birth and have children who were actually spawned from Him.

Although Adam and Eve did not serve this particular purpose, God's desire was nonetheless completed through them. Four thousand years down the road God used the heir of Adam and Eve to bring about His Son. God blended His creation with Him and brought forth an entirely new genetic code! Through Adam's spiritual death and the subsequent birth of Jesus, a unique hybrid came into being: A man God.

And he called her "woman"

Now a plant cannot be produced unless there exists a seed and an environment for growth. Conception and birth can only take place when a seed and a womb are involved. If God wanted a Son, then He had to plant His seed. God had a seed; the Word is the Seed of God.

In order for God to plant His seed, He needed a womb. When God created Adam, He created Him with a womb. God then said, "it is not good for man to be alone" and went on to separate the womb from the man by taking one of his ribs and forming a being whom Adam, not coincidentally, called "woman".

Adam must die

It was imperative that God orchestrate a way for Adam to die because, *"...what you sow is not made alive unless it dies." (1 Cor 15:36 NKJV)*. If God is a Sower and uses the laws of sowing and reaping to produce bigger and greater things, then it was necessary that God sow His created being in order to get His desired Son and sons.

With this information, God knew that without the law sin was dead and without sin there could be no death; hence He gave Adam a law with the penalty of a death sentence. God knew that Adam would break the law because of the material in which He had been made. There was no question that Adam would eat that fruit. It was in this way that God arranged Adam's death. God always knows what He is doing; no one has ever gotten out in front of Him. If anyone is the First and Above Only at all times, it is God.

A needful death

Death is an integral part of the very important cycle of resurrection life. Jesus was our example in this; He had to die before He could be resurrected and we must die before we can be resurrected, *"Therefore we are buried with him by baptism into death: that like as Christ was raised up from the dead by the glory of the Father, even so we also should walk in newness of life. For if we have been planted together in the likeness of his death, we shall be also in the likeness of his resurrection:" (Rom 6:4-5 KJV)*.

As Christians, we are planted together in the likeness of His death. Again we see a death -- a planting -- and then a resurrection. This is absolutely a major theme of the Bible. First Jesus and then us;

we were only continuing a pattern that God had instituted in creation: Adam lived, died, was buried, and lived again. Jesus lived, died, was buried, and lives forevermore. We live, die, are buried by baptism, and walk in eternal resurrection life.

The whole world is set up to exemplify this cycle. Plants drop seeds. These seeds die and then get buried in the earth, plants grow, seeds drop from these plants and die, get buried in the earth and become plants that grow.

In the same way, a human lives, and then he dies is buried and he lives again. He may live in heaven or he may live in hell, but his eternity begins the moment he dies. Everything lives, dies, goes back to the earth, and lives again, *"for dust thou art, and unto dust shalt thou return." In a moment, in the twinkling of an eye, at the last trump: for the trumpet shall sound, and the dead shall be raised incorruptible, and we shall be changed." (1 Cor 15:52 KJV)*

The womb

That being called *woman,* would eventually be used as the womb to carry the Seed of the Word of God. The very moment Adam sinned -- thus died spiritually, God spoke of his future Spawn Who would defeat sin, *"And I will put enmity between thee and the woman, and between thy seed and her seed; it shall bruise thy head, and thou shalt bruise his heel." (Gen 3:15 KJV).*

Look at how God uses the word "seed"! Adam sinned, died, and was planted and that is why God could speak these words. Adam's future harvest was now planted in the earth. Jesus was on His way. In the spiritual realm, the show is over. The Director of the drama always knows the end.

When Adam and Eve spiritually died, their seeds were planted in the spiritual realm so that God could bring forth His Son.

Immediately following, Adam planted his natural seed in Eve and the resulting children became the first in the physical bloodline that would lead to God's first Son. Now we have a spiritual seed planted and a natural seed planted and both will culminate in the life of Christ.

The First Begotten

Eventually the seed of God entered Mary's womb and a man-God was born just as God ordered in His curse against the serpent. This was the Son of God. Jesus was the first begotten of the Father. Jesus was never created. He was eternally existent in the spiritual realm and then born into the natural, *"And the Word was made flesh, and dwelt among us, (and we beheld his glory, the glory as of the only begotten of the Father,) full of grace and truth." (John 1:14 KJV)*.

When Jesus was born, God laid eyes on His very first child. During His life, Jesus was clearly called the *only* begotten Son of God. However, Jesus was not only the Son of God but also the Son of man. Adam sowed the natural seed, and God sowed the spiritual seed.

Jesus was a Son

Jesus was the first manifestation of God's plan to have children. That is why when God made a public declaration concerning Jesus, He said the following, *"This is my beloved Son, in whom I am well pleased." (Matt 3:17)*. A son is what God wanted, and a Son is what He got and He was well pleased about it.

However, God was not finished. Jesus was a Son; singular. God wanted sons; plural. This is why, when speaking of those who would receive salvation through Christ, Paul said the following, *"For whom he did foreknow, he also did predestinate to be conformed to the image of his Son, that he might be the firstborn among many brethren." (Rom 8:29 KJV).*

We see a very definite progression from Adam to us. Adam had to die so that God could plant him and bring forth the harvest of His Son. Then the Son had to die so that God could plant the Son and bring forth a harvest of *many* sons. As we are, *"...planted together in the likeness of his death, we shall be also in the likeness of his resurrection:"* Adam died, Jesus died, now we have to die, *"...that they might be called trees of righteousness, the planting of the LORD, that he might be glorified." (Isa 61:3b KJV).*

God orchestrated the death of Adam and placed him in a garden. God then orchestrated the death of His Son and placed Him in a garden, *"Now in the place where he was crucified there was a garden; and in the garden a new sepulchre...There laid they Jesus..." (John 19:41-42 KJV).*

Mary Magdaline came to the tomb of Jesus the morning of His resurrection. When she saw Jesus she thought He was the gardener. Adam was sown in a garden and Jesus was sown in a garden. As well, we are planted together with Him in His death. This wording tells us that the process of death brings forth resurrection life.

Even in His life, Jesus seemed to frequent a garden, *"When Jesus had spoken these words, he went forth with his disciples over the brook Cedron, where was a garden, into the which he entered, and his disciples. And Judas also, which betrayed him, knew the place: for Jesus ofttimes resorted thither with his disciples." (John 18:1-2 KJV).*

Jesus visited this garden with His disciples so often that Judas, who was one of the twelve disciples, knew exactly where to find Him. Jesus understood that He was a Seed and that He needed to be sown. A garden was the most natural place for Him to be.

This entire process was begun the moment Adam ate that fruit. Interestingly, it was sin that killed Adam and it was sin that crucified Christ. If Jesus had not taken on the sin of the world, He would not have died. All sin ends in death and Jesus had no sin of His own.

This progression of life, sin, death, and resurrection life will be continued until the whole earth is filled with the glory of the Lord. We cannot help but to notice a very definite pattern.

```
Sown in corruption; raised in incorruption
```

In the following account from the fifteenth chapter of 1 Corinthians, Paul is speaking to a group of people in the Corinthian church who did not believe in the resurrection of the dead.

Paul addresses this on two fronts. He begins by giving a detailed account of all the witnesses that actually saw Jesus alive on earth after He was crucified and then follows with, *"But if there be no resurrection of the dead, then is Christ not risen..."* Paul is telling them that they have no Gospel without resurrection.

Paul then tells these unbelievers that this life becomes pointless if there is no resurrection from the dead, *"If after the manner of men I have fought with beasts at Ephesus, what advantageth it me, if the dead rise not? let us eat and drink; for to morrow we die...If in this life only we have hope in Christ, we are of all men most miserable....But now is Christ risen from the dead, and become the firstfruits of them that slept."*

Finally we have come to the place where Paul instructs this church about how resurrection takes place. Read these passages carefully and slowly. This is the only significant teaching concerning Adam found in the New Testament and it just happens to be all about sowing a dead seed and reaping a supernatural harvest:

> *"For since by man came death, by man came also the resurrection of the dead....But some man will say, How are the dead raised up? and with what body do they come? Thou fool, that which thou sowest is not quickened, except it die: And that which thou sowest, thou sowest not that body that shall be, but bare grain, it may chance of wheat, or of some other grain: But God giveth it a body as it hath pleased him, and to every seed his own body."*

Since by Adam came death, by Adam also came resurrection. How does this happen and what sort of thing do we end up with? Don't you know?; that which you sow is not made alive unless it first dies. And the thing that is sown is not what it will spring forth to be, rather it is just a small piece of grain, possibly wheat. But God gave it the body He pleased to give it. Paul goes on:

> *"For as in Adam all die, even so in Christ shall all be made alive. So also is the resurrection of the dead. It is sown in corruption; it is raised in incorruption: It is sown in dishonour; it is raised in glory: it is sown in weakness; it is raised in power: It is sown a natural body; it is raised a spiritual body."*

Just as we all died in Adam, all who are in Christ are made alive. The resurrection of the dead is the same way; it is sown in corruption. The Greek word for "corruption" is "phthora" which means *decay and ruin*. The root word is "phtheiro" and means, *to shrivel or wither*. The seed was sown when it shriveled and withered in death, and then it was raised in incorruption in the exact same way that our mortal bodies will decay before we are ever raised to be with Him immortally.

The Greek word for incorruption is "aphtharsia" and means, *incorruptibility; generally unending existence...genuineness*

...immortality, incorruption, sincerity. Adam was sown in decay and ruin; Jesus was raised in incorruptibility. Adam was sown in death; Jesus was raised in immortality. Adam was sown a natural body, Jesus was raised a spiritual body.

> *"There is a natural body, and there is a spiritual body.*
> *And so it is written,*
> *The first man Adam was made a living soul;*
> *the last Adam was made a quickening spirit."*

The first man Adam was made a living soul, but the last Man Jesus was made a resurrecting spirit.

> *"Howbeit that was not first which is spiritual,*
> *but that which is natural;*
> *and afterward that which is spiritual.*
> *The first man is of the earth, earthy:*
> *the second man is the Lord from heaven.*
> *As is the earthy, such are they also that are earthy:*
> *and as is the heavenly,*
> *such are they also that are heavenly.*
> *And as we have borne the image of the earthy,*
> *we shall also bear the image of the heavenly."*

Adam was not spiritual; he was natural. It is what comes afterward that is spiritual. Adam was of the earth, "earthy" which, in Greek, means dusty or dirty. The root word is "choos" and means, *a heap (as poured out), that is, rubbish; lose dirt:—dust.* Adam was of the earth; dusty, dirty, rubbish. Jesus was the Lord from heaven.

As was Adam, so are we, and as is Jesus so do we become because, just as we bore the image of Adam, we shall also bear the image of Christ, *"as we have borne the image of the earthy, we shall also bear the image of the heavenly."*

This is the only time this word "earthy" is used in the New

Testament. The specific word *earthy*, meaning dusty, dirty, and rubbish, is *only* used to describe Adam.

> *"So when this corruptible*
> *shall have put on incorruption,*
> *and this mortal shall have put on immortality,*
> *then shall be brought to pass the saying that is written,*
> *Death is swallowed up in victory.*
> *O death, where is thy sting?*
> *O grave, where is thy victory?*
> *The sting of death is sin;*
> *and the strength of sin is the law.*
> *But thanks be to God, which giveth us the victory*
> *through our Lord Jesus Christ."*

From the foundation of the world

We can't miss this message. What I am seeing in our verses from 1 Corinthians is that Adam, the natural, had to be *sown* in order for Jesus, the spiritual, to be *raised*. God planted a dead seed and raised a spiritual harvest through His Son. God is a Sower and that means that sowing is what He does.

So, where do the many sons come in? Specifically, we come in through Jesus, *"According as he hath chosen us in him before the foundation of the world, that we should be holy and without blame before him in love: Having predestinated us unto the adoption of children by Jesus Christ to himself, according to the good pleasure of his will," (Eph 1:4-5 KJV)*. In the same way that Adam had to die before Jesus could be raised, so Jesus had to die before we could be raised. God is a Sower.

Before the foundation of the world, God chose us to be holy and without blame before Him in love. Not only this, but His plan involved us becoming His sons through Jesus, according to His good pleasure. The only way we can be holy and without blame before Him in love is to be born of Him through Christ.

Adam was no different; the only way he had any chance of becoming a son was through the salvation process. The only way Adam could be saved is if he had a need to be saved. And the only way Adam would have needed to be saved is if he sinned. God had a plan and that plan worked perfectly. Jesus was slain before Adam was created so that salvation was in place before sin was conceived. God was never caught off guard. The God of the Universe made a man in His image. He did not screw up.

Sevenfold

There are many ways that God increases us with His Word. We are instructed in Proverbs, *"...do not despise a thief, if he steal to satisfy his soul when he is hungry; But if he be found, he shall restore sevenfold; he shall give all the substance of his house. (6:30-31 KJV)*. This scripture is telling us not to blame a person if he takes something to satisfy his soul when he is hungry, but see that he return what he took sevenfold; he should give all the substance of his house if necessary. In this way, God increases the person who has something taken from him.

One of the most comforting things about God is that He plays by His own rules. You see, Jehovah Elohim increased us when He subjected us to vanity. In giving us back what He took from us, He had to give seven times over and all the substance of His house. There need never be bad news as long is God is involved; He knows how to make every bad thing better than it was before it went bad! Before Adam and Eve sinned, they were not even capable of receiving the level of blessing that God could only provide through Christ.

Not only did God increase us sevenfold, but He *did* give all the substance of His house; He gave Himself. God gave all that He had. This idea was beautifully explained to us through the parable of the pearl which is found in the thirteenth chapter of Matthew.

We aren't going to despise God because He took something from us to satisfy His soul when He was hungry. Well, we know He was hungry for sons! Apparently, sons would satisfy His soul. God took something from us to satisfy His soul. He took our ability to do well so that we would die and He could raise us as sons! Now, through Jesus, God has returned to us sevenfold and all the substance of His house.

God's whole purpose concerning us is wrapped up in Jesus. God never intended for Adam to stay in the garden! He had a much bigger plan. It was the plan of redemption. To *redeem* means to buy back. God sold us out because He wanted to buy us back.

This is why salvation was not offered to Satan; God didn't sell him out. However, God *formed* His humans in such a way as to produce a hell bent disposition and He operates within the perimeters of His own rules. If God sold us, then He had an obligation to buy us back. That is why it was all predestined before the foundation of the world. God never planned on anything else. God subjected us to vanity in order to deliver us and have sons. Our most magnificent Lord has had the control all along. How much easier to enter into His rest when we know that this kind of God is at the helm!

The law of increase

God made Adam of hell dust, let him die, buried him, and reaped the harvest of Jesus. Jesus was born of God through man, was crucified, died, was buried, and brought many sons to glory. That is the law of increase. God took something from us so that He could pay us back seven-fold and even give all the substance of His house. Due to God's actions, we are in a position to be better, have more, and experience more of God than the Garden of Eden ever offered. As we spend some time studying the benefits of this great and glorious plan, we will understand and appreciate why God did things the way He did.

Part(y) II
𝒯he 𝐵eauty

Free to be Holy

Introduction

Now that we have explored the logic which is found in our hell bent disposition, it is time to explore the beauty of it.

Have you ever clenched your fist with all your might for about one minute? You must do this. Start out by taking note of your hand. It is certainly just sitting there, or hanging there, or being used to hold this book. But, probably, you had not taken much notice of it before now.

Now form a tight fist and hold it with all your might for one full minute. You will have to continually retighten your grip, as your hand will instinctively try to relax. When the minute is up, slowly loosen your grip. Now you are really paying attention to your hand. Notice the complete feeling of release. It is somewhat euphoric when the pain, though still there, becomes overwhelmed by the glory of deliverance. Ahhh, I'm free.

The hand, which is normally quite mundane, suddenly becomes the star in a dramatic experience. The freedom to move, which the hand has always enjoyed, is now appreciated in a whole new way. Before the test, the hand felt neither good nor bad. During the test the hand felt stressed. After the test, the hand felt superb. Through this test, you have experienced a very small part of life in a whole new way.

God used sin to squeeze us forcefully for long enough to get us to thump on our breast and yell, "Uncle!" This was so that His sweet deliverance could be experienced in all of its glory. There is simply no way we can experience the fullness of good until we are willing to experience its counterpart: Evil.

The distance of wrath

We heard the bad news, now we are going to take some time to look at the beauty of the hell dust factor. To give you an idea of the degree of this beauty, I will share with you a concept I recently learned from God.

One morning I was communing with God in His Word and He kept telling me that I could have whatever I wanted. From Scripture to Scripture throughout the Bible the message was clear. "God", I finally said to Him, "You are so good to me; I don't even understand this kind of goodness." Shortly after that, I found myself in the book of Revelation. What I read there shocked me:

> *"...If any man worship the beast and his image, and receive his mark in his forehead, or in his hand, The same shall drink of the wine of the wrath of God, which is poured out without mixture into the cup of his indignation; and he shall be tormented with fire and brimstone in the presence of the holy angels, and in the presence of the Lamb: And the smoke of their torment ascendeth up for ever and ever: and they have no rest day nor night,..."*
> (Rev 14:9-11 KJV)

If I try very hard to think of the worst person in history, I still cannot picture myself being comfortable with watching his torment eternally. The wording in these verses is stunningly horrible. God's enemies will drink the wine of His wrath poured out without mixture into His cup. Full wrath: straight up. What a visual! I cannot even imagine the undiluted version of His wrath, let alone the full potency.

Who can watch?

"And he shall be tormented with fire and brimstone." I had watched a television program the night before about a burn victim. The show was very graphic. At times I had to close my eyes. To be tormented with fire and brimstone has to be the worst possible pain. Who can watch? Oddly, God can.

This torment went on *in the presence of the holy angels, and in the presence of the Lamb.* The entire host of heaven will eternally watch the torment of God's enemies, *"the smoke of their torment ascendeth up for ever and ever: and they have no rest day nor night."* There was no end to this suffering that was taking place right before the eyes of a company of angels and the very Son of God! How can we comprehend such a thing? With what can we compare it?

I don't get it

I said, "God, I don't get it. I am not good like You and yet, there is a goodness inside of me that would not want a person to suffer at all, much less have the smoke of their torment before me forever! I don't understand this. It sounds terrible to me."

You're right; you don't get it

"Neither do you understand my goodness." was God's reply to me. As I sat and pondered that, I was reminded of the book <u>Mere Christianity</u>. A passage from this classic by C.S. Lewis spoke of the concept of good and evil, *"The better stuff a creature is made of -- the cleverer, stronger, and freer it is --then the better it will be if it goes right, so also the worse it will be if it goes wrong. A Cow cannot be very good or very bad; a dog can be both better and worse; a child better and worse still; an ordinary man, still more so; a man of genius, still more so; a superhuman spirit, best -- or worst -- of all."*

Because God is a superhuman spirit, He is best and worst of all. He is called a terrible God and that He is. He will either be your best friend or your worst enemy, but, rest assured, He will be one of the two. He is best and worst of all.

Not in the path of wrath

Now, this "worst of all" part should not be a concern to us. The wrath of God is poured out on His enemies; not His children, *"For God hath not appointed us to wrath, but to obtain salvation by our Lord Jesus Christ" (1Thes 5:9)*. The enemies get the "worst of all" part of God; we get the "best of all" part of God.

The whole point God had when He showed me this verse was in getting me to see His vast goodness in a way that I could more easily measure it. If God's wrath is so appalling that it makes my stomach turn, then how great is His goodness? Now that is something to think about. God is always better than we think He is. That is because our finite minds do not have the capacity to absorb this information, *"For as the heavens are higher than the earth, so are my ways higher than your ways, and my thoughts than your thoughts." (Isa 55:9 KJV)*.

Free to be Holy

> A man might as well hope to hold the north wind in the hollow of his hand as expect to control by his own strength those boisterous powers which dwell within his fallen nature. This is a greater feat than any of the fabled labors of Hercules: God is wanted here.
> **All of Grace, C. H. Spurgeon**

Sin; a necessary evil

It was necessary for Adam to die; therefore it was necessary for Adam to sin. Sin was a necessary evil. But, as is customary for Him, God had even more in mind. Not only was sin necessary in causing the death of the seed, it was also necessary in nurturing that seed.

Jesus told a parable of a fig tree, *"He spake also this parable; A certain man had a fig tree planted in his vineyard; and he came and sought fruit thereon, and found none. Then said he unto the dresser of his vineyard, Behold, these three years I come seeking fruit on this fig tree, and find none: cut it down; why cumbereth it the ground? And he answering said unto him, Lord, let it alone this year also, till I shall dig about it, and dung it: And if it bear fruit, well: and if not, then after that thou shalt cut it down."* (Luke 13:6-9 KJV).

The Lord of this vineyard planted a seed and as that seed came up and became a plant, He began to look for fruit. When he didn't see fruit, he commanded that the plant be cut down. However, the "dresser" (Greek "worker") of the vine, whom I believe typifies the Holy Spirit Who is working with us, convinced the Lord to give Him a year to take cuts at the root base and throw some manure into it. The "dresser" of the vine added that if the tree didn't bear fruit after this, then it should be cut down.

God's way of producing fruit in our lives is through cutting at the root of our being and throwing in the worst possible thing: Manure. Our trials tend to hit us right where we live.

It is a known fact that people are drawn to God more in adversity than in peace. The more intense our battle, the quicker we will drop to our knees. The battle, which is the result of the curse, is what turns us toward the God of deliverance. Adam died, was sown, and then was cut and dunged through the curse. Now he needs a Deliverer. In our adversity, we need a Deliverer. Sin was, and is a necessary evil.

Penetrating the darkness

Beauty is found in the highs and the lows, the ins and the outs, and the ups and the downs. We look at majestic mountain peaks not even taking into consideration the role of the valley below. A mountain is only as high as the valley is low: The higher the valley, the less ominous the peak.

When I look into my shade garden I see a wonderful array of diffused light. The shadows are deep and are occasionally stabbed by sharp glimpses of light. When a breeze causes the sun's rays to jump and flit about, it is as though there are crystals in the air. This area of the garden is much more entertaining than my sunny garden. The sunny garden's beauty depends entirely on the plants themselves. The shady garden has plants *and* a light show.

The Las Vegas strip is interesting by day but breathtaking by night. The moon, though barely visible by day, becomes mesmerizing as it is cloaked in the darkness of night. Fireworks are used at night because the dark sky provides the perfect backdrop for their beauty. The garden, the Las Vegas strip, the moon, and the fireworks do not change, however, they become much more beautiful simply because of their contrasting background.

In the same way that darkness can be very instrumental in showcasing light, the darkness of sin can be very instrumental in showcasing the light of the goodness of God. On the first day of creation God created the light of goodness and then separated it from the evil of darkness. God continued and made an earth and trees. Now we have a shady garden showcasing a breathtaking, mesmerizing Beauty.

Stories amidst the sin

The Bible is considered by some to be the most beautiful piece of literature ever written. Its beauty is found in the way God relates to mankind right in the middle of the evil of sin. God does not have skeletons in His closet; He lets it all hang out because He is not ashamed. Things are going along as planned. Let's take a walk in one of God's shade gardens and enjoy His light show:

"I waited patiently for the LORD; and he inclined unto me, and heard my cry. He brought me up also out of an horrible pit, out of the miry clay, and set my feet upon a rock, and established my goings. And he hath put a new song in my mouth, even praise unto our God: many shall see it, and fear, and shall trust in the LORD. Blessed is that man that maketh the LORD his trust, and respecteth not the proud, nor such as turn aside to lies. Many, O LORD my God, are thy wonderful works which thou hast done, and thy thoughts which are to us-ward: they cannot be reckoned up in order unto thee: if I would declare and speak of them, they are more than can be numbered. Withhold not thou thy tender mercies from me, O LORD: let thy lovingkindness and thy truth continually preserve me. For innumerable evils have compassed me about: mine iniquities have taken hold upon me, so that I am not able to look up; they are more than the hairs of mine head: therefore my heart faileth me. Be pleased, O LORD, to deliver me: O LORD, make haste to help me. Let them be ashamed and confounded together that seek after my soul to destroy it; let them be driven backward and put to shame that wish me evil. Let them be desolate for a reward of their shame that say unto me, Aha, aha. Let all those that seek thee rejoice and be glad in thee: let such as love thy salvation say continually, The LORD be magnified. But I am poor and needy; yet the Lord thinketh upon me: thou art my help and my deliverer; make no tarrying, O my God."
(Psa 40:1-5 & 11-17 KJV)

We can feel the heart of this psalmist. David does not merely exist; he lives. He isn't just going through the motions of life and he isn't taking a stroll in a garden. Rather, David has this very intimate, viable relationship with a magnificent God. David is squarely in the middle of trouble *and* sin, yet, what we notice in his words is the love and trust he has in his God. How can this kind of passion manifest without the aspect of sin?

Deliverance unto holiness

If we want to walk in the righteousness of God, Isaiah instructs us to look to the God Who delivered us from our "pit", *"Hearken to me, ye that follow after righteousness, ye that seek the LORD: look unto the rock whence ye are hewn, and to the hole of the pit whence ye are digged." (Isa 51:1 KJV)*. If we are going after righteousness, we are told to look to the "Rock" Who made us, and the hole of the pit from which He saved us. As we keep our eyes on the God Who delivered us, and keep this deliverance in our mind, our faith will be strengthened and we will be better able to trust Him for our righteousness.

According to the psalmist, it is the deliverance from our pit that puts a new song in our heart. It is our testimony of this deliverance that teaches us to trust in God. It is this trust that empowers us to stay close to God. As we abide with Him through our trials we are comforted by the many thoughts God has toward us.

It is the fact that we must be preserved which causes us to appreciate God's loving kindness and tender mercies. It is the innumerable evils around us and our own iniquities that are so heavy we cannot even look up and so plenteous that they are like the hairs of our head that make God's deliverance so sweet. The darkness of sin showcases the goodness of God, *"...the Lord thinketh upon me: thou art my help and my deliverer...".* Sin is a necessary evil.

The greatest story ever told

This thing that God has drawn us into has the potential to be greater than anything we have seen on the big screen. God wants to get in there and tangle with us in this unbelievable production, (comedy, tragedy, love story…you name it) called, *Life with Him and sin*.

In order to take an active role in this drama, we must not only accept the drama, but accept the fact that it was orchestrated by God. God is a drama King; He loves drama. The presence of sin forced the issue of deliverance. Everything was set up so that one cannot be good or receive goodness if it not be by Godly deliverance and provision. God has left us with no choice. We must look to Him. Our God, the Deliverer, is just waiting to dive into our darkness and rescue us.

Rescued from a pit

When my children were very young God assured me that each of them would be saved. I was very thankful for this assurance, but I had a small concern. I did not want my children to grow up clean, clueless Christians. I wanted them to understand the love of God in a deep and real way. Having said that, I also did not want to lose my children for even a minute. So I prayed to God, "Do whatever You have to do to make sure my children experience You in all of Your glory. Just please, let me always be by their side no matter what they have to go through."

God honored my request. Although we have been through many serious trials as a family, and many ugly roads have been trod, we have never been emotionally distant from one another. We saw many miracles in the darkest of hours and these have bonded us closely. The following is one story illustrating this.

Not long after my son, Nathan, moved to another state, he found himself in a very large and deep pit. Nathan had been addicted to drugs, homeless, jobless, and without a vehicle for weeks when he called me and told me that he was now being chased by police and a man was seeking his life.

Due to the fact that his life had been heading in this direction for a while, all I could do at this pivotal moment is do as I had always done and turn him toward the God of deliverance. It had been some time since Nathan had taken my words seriously, however, this night would prove to change his course.

What should I do?

Nathan feared going to the police about this man's threats because the police had been told lies and he knew they were after him as well. Nathan had no vehicle, no money, no job, and no place to lay his head; he was a true vagabond in a hopeless situation.

I tried to encourage my son as I assured him that the God of the Bible would avenge him of his enemies. Even I was getting bored with this speech. I wasn't ignorant of my son's sins, and I knew that much of his situation was due to his own wrong choices. However, I also knew that the same God Who could rescue Nathan from his problems, could also rescue him from his sins. "When will he understand this?" I wondered.

Got it!

For some reason, this time was different than the rest. The moment I told my son that God would avenge him of his enemies he received that information into his heart and made it his Truth. I didn't realize this was happening at the time. However, I knew something had happened because I noticed a change in his tone.

When I went on to advise Nathan concerning whether or not he should go to the police, he interrupted me and said my words back to me, "God will take care of it." That was the end of that. I had a meeting so we agreed to talk again later. Before he hung up the phone he asked me to find Scriptures for him concerning what I had told him.

Deliverance

With the speed of lightning, Nathan's deliverance began. The man who was threatening my son's life had been calling him regularly, using vile insults to tempt him to come to his house. He had even called me and used vulgarity to insult me, hoping to entice my son. This man was actually keeping a rifle next to his front door.

You see, this man had told the police that Nathan had robbed his garage. Therefore, he was doing everything in his power to get my son to come on his property so he would have a reason to kill him in feigned self-defense. He had openly stated to Nathan and to others that he was going to shoot him dead.

Shortly after we got off the phone this man called Nathan again. However, this time he got more than he bargained for. Because Nathan had made the decision to trust God to avenge him, things went a bit different.

When the man began to spew his venom, my son stopped him and said, "I rebuke you in the name of Jesus." The man began to laugh. Nathan saw this for what it was and added, "You are in big trouble. I feel sorry for you", and then hung up the phone.

Nathan knew that God was going to avenge him of his enemies. In his book, that meant that this man who laughed at the name of Jesus was in line for the wrath of God. He felt sorry for him. This man never called Nathan again and that was a long time ago. The last we heard, he was doing time for battery. However, it matters not. He is no longer a factor in Nathan's life.

Instant results

My son got instant results when he took God at His Word. I could tell things were different when we spoke again later that evening. After Nathan told me about his final run in with this man, I shared some Scriptures that I had found concerning the avenging of his enemies. This time, instead of just agreeing to read them, Nathan wanted me to read them to him. I gladly did this.

Reading the Scriptures gave way to a spiritual flow between us that was uninterrupted for several hours as we spoke. We only ended the conversation because our phones were going dead. This had never happened before; it was evident to me that Nathan was avenged of his enemies from without *and* from within.

Nathan was delivered from that man, but more importantly, he was delivered from himself. Later that night, Nathan took the Scriptures and read them to himself before he fell asleep on the floor of an abandoned apartment. A Bible was one of the few things he had left in his possession.

Bam! Bam! Bam!

The next day, mind you, after months of unemployment, Nathan was offered a construction job. He began working that day. At that job my son met a Christian man who lived two doors down from the boss who daily picked him up for work. This same man had a room for rent in his house.

This quick sequence of events changed my son's position entirely. In the space of twenty-four hours Nathan went from being homeless, jobless, without transportation, penniless, pursued, threatened, and falsely accused, to having a job, a nice home, a daily, free ride to work, and a Christian friend who promptly took him to his church. All of this ended up relocating Nathan from the area where he was being pursued, into a safe neighboring county where no one even knew him. Nathan was given a clean slate. Today Nathan owns his own business in that town. Pretty nifty.

Before I was aware of this news, I had stumbled upon the eighteenth Psalm. As I read it, I knew God was speaking to me concerning Nathan. I was anxious to encourage him with it when he called. However, before I had a chance to tell him, Nathan told me what had just happened that day. I about fell out of my chair. I said to him, "Honey, I thought I was going to give you a Psalm that would guide you, but the Psalm I have to give you describes the very thing that just happened to you!" He was anxious to hear.

Psalm 18 (part of it anyway)

Let me share with you the Psalm God had given to me concerning Nathan from the New Living Translation of the Bible:

> "I love you, LORD; you are my strength.
> The LORD is my rock, my fortress,
> and my savior;
> my God is my rock, in whom I find protection.
> He is my shield, the strength of my salvation,
> and my stronghold.
> I will call on the LORD, who is worthy of praise,
> for he saves me from my enemies.
> **The ropes of death surrounded me;**
> **the floods of destruction swept over me.**
> **The grave wrapped its ropes around me;**
> **death itself stared me in the face.**
> **But in my distress I cried out to the LORD;**
> **yes, I prayed to my God for help.**
> He heard me from his sanctuary;
> my cry reached his ears.
> Then the earth quaked and trembled;
> the foundations of the mountains shook;
> they quaked because of his anger.

Smoke poured from his nostrils;
fierce flames leaped from his mouth;
glowing coals flamed forth from him.
He opened the heavens and came down;
dark storm clouds were beneath his feet.
Mounted on a mighty angel, he flew,
soaring on the wings of the wind.
He shrouded himself in darkness,
veiling his approach with dense rain clouds.
The brilliance of his presence
broke through the clouds,
raining down hail and burning coals.
The LORD thundered from heaven;
the Most High gave a mighty shout.
He shot his arrows and scattered his enemies;
his lightning flashed, and they were greatly confused.
Then at your command, O LORD,
at the blast of your breath,
the bottom of the sea could be seen,
and the foundations of the earth were laid bare.
He reached down from heaven and rescued me;
he drew me out of deep waters.
He delivered me from my powerful enemies, from
those who hated me and were too strong for me.
They attacked me at a moment when I was weakest,
but the LORD upheld me.
He led me to a place of safety;
he rescued me because he delights in me."

My son got to live this Psalm. Nathan is not clueless concerning God's love and glory. He got to experience the sweet taste of victory. Nathan's Dad came storming down from heaven to avenge him of his enemies (within as well as without). God reached down and rescued him; He drew him out of deep water. God delivered my son from his powerful enemies who hated him and were too strong for him. Satan got at him while Nathan was weak, but the Lord sustained him. God led my son to a place of safety. God rescued Nathan simply because he loved him.

```
Gifts along the way
```

This great deliverance contained unexpected blessings; one of them is quite entertaining. Before Nathan's deliverance came, he had a rap sheet a mile long. A friend had helped Nathan look it up on the Internet. Together, they found Nathan, and a lengthy list of his past legal discrepancies and their ensuing consequences. In addition to the debts he had already paid to society, there were tickets, unpaid bills, and outstanding judgments of which he had not been aware.

About two weeks after his deliverance Nathan visited the friend who had helped him find his on-line rap sheet. He shared with this friend how God had come in and saved the day. She was leery, to say the least. Nathan was undaunted, "I'll prove it! Look me up."

```
Somehow he knew
```

Now this was a real faith move on Nathan's part because he had no idea what his friend was going to find. He did not have a computer and had no natural way of knowing what may or may not have happened to his cyber-world list of sins. However, through God's deliverance, Nathan had learned to trust Him for everything.

Just as he had thought, Nathan's friend found him as she did before only this time there was no list. Nathan's cyber-world criminal profile had been miraculously wiped clean. What a magnificent God. How can we comprehend such grand love? His loving kindness is everlasting and His mercy endures forever.

A few weeks after this incident I ran across an entry in my prayer journal that I had written several months before when I saw that Nathan was heading for deep waters. I was amazed by the fulfillment of each request. I'd like to share it with you:

9-6-05:

> *Holy Spirit help me pray. I love you. Father, Nathan is in trouble. I ask that you protect him from the world. I ask that you cause him to become involved in the church you would like him to be involved in. I pray that you rescue him from all drug use. He is my son and I am righteous because you made me righteous by taking on my sin. Your Word says the children of the righteous shall prosper. Thank you so much for that. Keep him safe and speak to his heart through the Holy Spirit you put inside of him. Keep your hedge about Nathan and let the truthful words he has heard of you in the past begin to take firm root in his heart. Protect his personal body, his mind, and his belongings. I expect satan to repay him everything he has stolen from him sevenfold. Bring him into you as only you can. I am trusting you with him. Give him your knowledge and wisdom and watch over him without ceasing. I give him over into your care. I pray this in the eternally powerful name of Jesus. Amen.*

Nathan had been gloriously delivered *from* the bondage of corruption *into* the glorious liberty of the children of God. All drug usage ceased, but more than that, Nathan began to live in wisdom and power. Everything he had ever learned about God came flooding back to him. Nathan's life became a daily testimony of trust and deliverance.

In the months following his dramatic deliverance, Nathan and I would spend literally hours on the phone pouring over Scriptures and sharing wisdom and testimonies with one another. It was as though someone turned a light on inside of him, and indeed, that Someone did. Nathan looked to his God of deliverance and the pit

Free to be Holy

from which he had been digged and he found the righteousness of God.

```
"And they overcame him by the blood of the
Lamb, and by the word of their testimony"
```

This will forever be a standout time for my son. What a powerful testimony to have hidden in your heart when your faith needs a boost! If God can do that, He can do anything. What an exciting time! The children of Israel were constantly reminded by God to remember their great deliverance from Egypt. Would that glorious deliverance have been possible without the element of sin? No. Is that kind of excitement even plausible without the element of sin? I don't think so.

In order for Nathan to experience this glorious deliverance, he had to be in a position to *need* a glorious deliverance. Now Nathan knows Who God is. He doesn't know because he read it in a book, or because God sat down with him one day and told him what a great God He was. He knows because he lived it.

Nathan was picked up, he was delivered from a habit he had carried for years, he was rescued from a man who was seeking his life and others who wanted to imprison him, and he was placed in a safe habitation with transportation and income. Sin was a necessary evil. There is literally no better way for a person to understand the length of God's goodness.

> *"That ye...May be able to comprehend with all saints*
> *what is the breadth, and length, and depth, and height;*
> *And to know the love of Christ, which passeth knowledge,..."*

```
He is Who He is
```

As I said before, the spiritual realm is not a transitional place. God does not morph from one thing to another. When God wanted a human, He created one; He did not become one. When God wanted a Son, He planted His seed into a human and grew a Son; God did not morph into a son. In this same light, God did not morph into a Savior because we suddenly needed a Savior.

God is not a doer He is a be-er. "God is"; a very short sentence that says it all. God is. When Moses asked God what he should tell the children of Israel concerning Who it was Who was sending him to deliver them, God told Moses to tell them that "I AM" sent him. God did not hand Moses a grocery list of things He was going to do, He simply said, "I AM". In other words, God was saying that He was going to act out all the things that He was.

The names of God

There are many and varied names of God. God's name is of utmost importance to Him. When teaching His disciples how to pray, Jesus began by saying, *"Our Father, Who art in heaven, hallowed be Thy name."* Let's look at some of these names of God as I take them from the first three volumes of a book series entitled, <u>Names of God</u> by Marilyn Hickey:

Elohim; the powerful and sovereign God.
Jehovah; the Giver, Sustainer, and Revealer of Life
El-Shaddai; the all sufficient One.
Adonai; the Master and Owner of all.
Jehovah Jireh; the unchanging Provider.
Jehovah M'Kaddesh; the One Who Sanctifies.
Jehovah Nissi; the Banner, or the One Who goes before.
Jehovah Rophe; the God Who heals.
Jehovah Shalom; the God Who gives peace.
Jehovah Tsidkenu; the God of our righteousness.
Jehovah Rohi; the God Who shepherds.
Jehovah Shammah; the God Who is present.
El Elyon; the Mighty One, Most High.
Jehovah Tsebaoth; the Lord of Hosts.
Jehovah Makkeh; the Lord our Smiter.

The reason that God has described His acts by His many names is because God is what He does. There is no separation between Who God is and what He does. What God does is nothing more than a natural outpouring of Who He is. God is the only truly genuine Being.

Savior

Jesus did not have to become a Savior as the result of Adam's sin. The book of Hebrews says that Jesus is the same yesterday, today, and forever. Jesus already was a Savior as He was slain from the foundation of the world. The name "Jesus" means "God saves." God is a Savior, which means that God did not merely save mankind because he found him in need of salvation, God saved mankind because God is a Savior and saving is what Saviors do.

God did not morph into a Savior when Adam sinned. Because God is Who He is, and He is Who He has always been, and He is Who He will always be, He says in Malachi, *"For I am the LORD, I change not..." (Mal 3:6 KJV)*. God could not have lived out the life of Jesus if mankind had not sinned. Before Adam sinned, there was no need for a Lamb Who had been slain.

When we look back at our list of the names of God we must ask ourselves, how many of God's names would never be able to see the light of day without sin?

All Powerful

Would we need power without sin? Power to do what? Does a perfect being need "all mighty power" to go about his business and replenish the earth in a perfect environment? Seems to me like one could do this task with a blindfold and a bum leg. When describing God's power the Hebrew word is defined as *valor, victory, force, mastery, might, mighty (act, power), power, strength*. An All Powerful God would be rather limited in the Garden of Eden.

Sustainer

If Jehovah was Adam's Sustainer, what was He sustaining? God had made Adam perfectly in His very own image and placed him in a perfect environment. It sounds to me like God made Adam *self-sustaining*. As long as Adam didn't eat that fruit, he stood just fine on his own. Jehovah, the Sustainer is not needed here.

Healer

Jehovah Rophe is the God Who heals. If Adam remained perfect in a perfect environment, why would he ever have need of healing? Wouldn't a perfect earth and a perfect man jive perfectly together? God, the Healer, is not needed here.

Imputer of Righteousness

Before Adam ate of that fruit, He was righteous. If Adam had not been righteous, he would not have been able to remain in the garden. It was only after he ate the fruit that Adam became unrighteous. Why would Adam need God's righteousness as long as he had a righteousness of his own? One might argue that Adam had Jehovah Tsidkenu, the God of our righteousness, before he sinned. If Adam had God's righteousness, he would not have been able to sin. God's righteousness does not fail. Before sin entered, Jehovah Tsidkenu, the God of our righteousness, was not needed.

Shepherd

Sheep are very dumb animals. The mentioning of any type of "flock" never brings up connotations of intelligence. Flocks are generally of low brain mobility. As a matter of fact, they are known for very stupid behaviors.

One day, after dropping off a friend, my son and I had an interesting interaction with a small herd of cows in a neighboring field. As we pulled out and headed down the driveway, we stared into the faces of about twelve cows that were practically climbing on top of one another to get a good look at us. These cows were absolutely intent on us.

We progressed slowly down the driveway toward them while the cows remained fixed. When we got to the street, we were just ten feet away from them. They stood still. The minute we turned onto the road, the entire herd began to run the fence line, trying to keep up with our car. They did this until they got to the end of their field and then they stopped and went about their business. Evidently these cows had been watching too many dogs.

Whenever there is the mention of a shepherd, there is also the idea of a flock. Without a flock, there is no need of a shepherd. If Adam had remained perfect and filled the earth with his perfect offspring and they remained perfect and everything remained perfect throughout eternity, where would we find a group of wanderers needing a Shepherd? The Lord our Shepherd is not needed here.

Lord of Hosts

Jehovah Tsebaoth, the Lord of Hosts, is the One Who will do battle for us. Literally, this name for God means, "to organize a mass of persons for war." This God, Who has been from eternity and Who will be throughout eternity, is preparing for war.

Would Adam have ever been in any sort of warfare if he had not eaten that fruit? With what would Adam contend? Where were his enemies necessitating an army? Perfect man + perfect world = no enemy. Throughout the entire account of Adam's pre-sin life we see only one time that Adam found himself in a situation where *it would appear* that he needed the Lord of Hosts: In his battle against sin.

Didn't Adam need the power of God to withstand the wiles of the devil? Only if that was God's plan. If eating that fruit was going to interfere with God's foreordained plan for man, the Lord of Hosts would have stepped in and battled for Adam; God is always where He is needed. However, the Lord of Hosts was not even in the vicinity, *"And the LORD God called unto Adam, and said unto him, Where art thou?"*

God knew exactly what was going on in the garden. There is no battle unless things are going awry. Things were not going awry; actually, they were going along rather well. Coming against the temptation of the serpent was not a battle; it was the *beginning* of a battle.

This would explain why our main heroes aren't giving us much of a show. Here the devil is having his one big moment in history and God isn't anywhere around while Adam simply opens his mouth and eats without so much as a raised eyebrow, "Mmmmm....fruit good."

If the Lord of Hosts had been present, evil would not have won this battle. Adam was righteous before he ate the fruit. If Adam were facing a battle needing to be won, God would have made sure He stood with His righteous man to do battle for him just as He does for us. But He did not. No, the Lord of Hosts was not needed in the garden.

Smiter

God said to Ezekiel, *"ye shall know that I am the LORD that smiteth."* The Hebrew word for "smiteth" is "nakah" and means, *to strike (lightly or severely, literally or figuratively, beat, cast forth, clap, give [wounds], go forward, indeed, kill, make [slaughter], murderer, punish, slaughter, slay, smite, strike, be stricken, (give) stripes, surely, wound.* I really don't see a role for this God to play in the perfect Garden of Eden. No, Jehovah Makkeh, the Lord our Smiter, could not be active before sin.

God is needed here

We cannot reverse what God has done. Only God has the power to reverse what He has done. How can God do a thing and then expect us to undo that very thing? That is ridiculous. It was God who placed us under the authority of the sin nature, and it is therefore God Who must deliver us from it. God is all that He is so that He could be everything we need. God needed sin in order for Him to act out His very nature.

I can no more remove the sun than remove my sinful disposition. As Spurgeon said, *"It is like taming the Leviathan, God is needed here."* That is the whole point; thanks to sin, God All Powerful, God the Sustainer, God the Healer, God the Imputer of Righteousness, God the Shepherd, God the Lord of Hosts, and God the Smiter is needed here. Hallelujah! What better way to get to know our magnificent God in all of His glory?

Good news for the sinner

We must always consider the audience when listening to the sermons of Jesus. The fifteenth chapter of Luke opens to introduce us to the audience at hand, *"Then drew near unto him all the publicans and sinners for to hear him."* Evidently Jesus was not throwing down a lot of "Thou shalts" and "Thou shalt nots" or He wouldn't be drawing a crowd of thieves and sinners in general. No, Jesus was preaching the glory of salvation to lost souls. His message came to these people like rain on dry ground. They loved Jesus and the message of hope that He preached.

Bad news for the scribe

And then there were those on the edge of the audience who did not think they were sinners at all, *"And the Pharisees and scribes murmured, saying, This man receiveth sinners, and eateth with them."* The scribes and Pharisees differentiated between themselves and those who were hanging out with Jesus. By calling these men sinners, the scribes and Pharisees were calling themselves righteous.

Now Jesus has two audiences: The Publicans and the sinners, and the scribes and the Pharisees. One group is drawn to Jesus while the other group is repelled by Him. One group is listening while the other group murmurs. One group draws near while the other stays in the periphery. Jesus was a Master Orator. Watch how He preaches to His entire audience in the following taken from the New Living Translation of the Bible:

Lost, found, and celebration

> *"If you had one hundred sheep, and one of them strayed away and was lost in the wilderness, wouldn't you leave the ninety-nine others to go and search for the lost one until you found it? And then you would joyfully carry it home on your shoulders."*

Jesus gave an illustration of how a natural man would leave ninety-nine sheep to look for one lost sheep. When he finds it, he brings it home on his shoulders like a victory march after a battle. Once back home, a triumphant celebration is in order:

> *"When you arrived, you would call together your friends and neighbors to rejoice with you because your lost sheep was found. In the same way, heaven will be happier over one lost sinner who returns to God than over ninety-nine others who are righteous and haven't strayed away!"*

Heaven will be happier over one lost sinner who returns to God over ninety-nine others who are righteous and have not strayed away. I'm sorry; I had to repeat that. Heaven was happier over Nathan when he returned to God than before he ever strayed away. No doubt the lost Publicans and sinners loved this sermon while the never-straying Pharisees grew more irate. Jesus goes on:

> *"Or suppose a woman has ten valuable silver coins and loses one. Won't she light a lamp and look in every corner of the house and sweep every nook and cranny until she finds it? And when she finds it, she will call in her friends and neighbors to rejoice with her because she has found her lost coin."*

Here we have a woman who will look in every corner and sweep every nook and cranny until she finds one lost coin. Though her circumstances *before* she lost the coin and *after* she found the coin were identical, the woman went from apathy to celebration, *"...when she finds it, she will call in her friends to rejoice with her...In the same way, there is joy in the presence of God's angels when even one sinner repents."* It is no wonder the sinners were drawn to Jesus; a party awaited their arrival!

The same, yet different

Nathan was a child of God before he fell into sin and he was a child of God after he was delivered from sin. His circumstances were the same before and after, yet there was joy in the presence of God's angels when Nathan repented. Heaven threw a party. God is a God of deliverance and there will be celebration when this deliverance manifests.

Since the scribes and Pharisees did not consider themselves to be sinners, this parable did not promise them a celebratory party in Heaven! There they sat with all of their laws and they didn't even get a mention. These parables offered hope to the lost while they afforded nothing to the never lost. The Pharisees were probably thinking, "What about the ninety-nine sheep and the nine coins? What are you going to do for them?" Those who do not acknowledge their complete wretchedness cannot comprehend the glory of deliverance.

The prodigal son

> "To illustrate the point further, Jesus told them this story: "A man had two sons. The younger son told his father, 'I want my share of your estate now, instead of waiting until you die.' So his father agreed to divide his wealth between his sons.
>
> "A few days later this younger son packed all his belongings and took a trip to a distant land, and there he wasted all his money on wild living. About the time his money ran out, a great famine swept over the land, and he began to starve. He persuaded a local farmer to hire him to feed his pigs. The boy became so hungry that even the pods he was feeding the pigs looked good to him. But no one gave him anything.
>
> "When he finally came to his senses, he said to himself, 'At home even the hired men have food enough to spare, and here I am, dying of hunger! I will go home to my father and say, "Father, I have sinned against both heaven and you, and I am no longer worthy of being called your son. Please take me on as a hired man."'

"So he returned home to his father. And while he was still a long distance away, his father saw him coming. Filled with love and compassion, he ran to his son, embraced him, and kissed him. His son said to him, 'Father, I have sinned against both heaven and you, and I am no longer worthy of being called your son.'

"But his father said to the servants, 'Quick! Bring the finest robe in the house and put it on him. Get a ring for his finger, and sandals for his feet. And kill the calf we have been fattening in the pen. We must celebrate

*with a feast, for this son of mine was dead and has now
returned to life. He was lost, but now he is found.'
So the party began.*

*"Meanwhile, the older son was in the fields working.
When he returned home, he heard music and dancing
in the house, and he asked one of the servants what
was going on. 'Your brother is back,' he was told, 'and
your father has killed the calf we were fattening and
has prepared a great feast. We are celebrating because
of his safe return.'*

*"The older brother was angry and wouldn't go in. His
father came out and begged him, but he replied, 'All
these years I've worked hard for you and never once
refused to do a single thing you told me to. And in all
that time you never gave me even one young goat for a
feast with my friends. Yet when this son of yours comes
back after squandering your money on prostitutes, you
celebrate by killing the finest calf we have.'*

*"His father said to him, 'Look, dear son, you and I are
very close, and everything I have is yours. We had to
celebrate this happy day. For your brother was dead
and has come back to life!
He was lost, but now he is found!'"*
(Luke 15:1 - 32 NLT)

```
It is better to have lost and loved than
never to have loved at all.
```

We are beginning to understand why the scribes and Pharisees wanted to kill Jesus on a regular basis. Jesus did not come with good news to those who were comfortable in their level of righteousness. A Pharisee was generally high on the mountain peak of self-reliance. As long as he was up there, he didn't need the valley talk. What the Pharisees needed was a reality check and while Jesus offered it up beautifully, they didn't receive it well.

When we look at these parables, we see a definite theme. God rejoices more over one who has been lost and found than in all the others who were never lost. I understand why God would rejoice over the one who had been found, but why was He not rejoicing equally over the ones who had never been lost? Weren't they the "good" ones? Shouldn't God be rejoicing at least as much over those who remain "good" than the one who went bad and then came back?

If behavior was what God was all about, then yes, He should be rejoicing more over those who remain "good" than those who fail and have to be rescued. However, God is not about behavior, He is about relationship. If God was all about behavior, He wouldn't have subjected mankind to vanity. Goodness is of no value unless it issues from God. We sin and then we are lost. We cry out and then we are found.

This very process is what forges deep relationships. Therefore, when we are lost and then found, a relationship is forged and we have something to celebrate.

Adam

"Heaven will be happier over one lost sinner who returns to God than over ninety-nine others who are righteous and haven't strayed away." What this tells us is that God rejoiced more over Adam's return after he ate the fruit than he did before the fruit was eaten. Jesus had already been slain, therefore Adam's deliverance was already in place. The moment Adam ate that fruit, the hunt began, *"And the LORD God called unto Adam, and said unto him, Where art thou?"* God found His man.

God is a Shepherd. It did not matter whether he was the first of the flock or the ninety-ninth, when Adam sinned he needed a Shepherd to bring him home. This Shepherd would find him, place him on His shoulders in a victory march, and then throw a party in heaven.

The good son

Before Adam sinned, he was the "good" son who didn't leave his Father. All that God had was Adam's and their relationship was just fine. Very much like the "good" son from our parable, Adam was apathetic concerning his blessings. We saw this evidenced in his lack of fight against temptation.

Although the "good" son from our parable had all the blessings of his father, he still found reason to complain, *"All these years I've worked hard for you and never once refused to do a single thing you told me to. And in all that time you never gave me even one young goat for a feast with my friends..."* His father answered him and said, *"Look, dear son, you and I are very close, and everything I have is yours."*

Although the good son had every good thing at his disposal, he didn't appreciate it the way his prodigal brother now did. His brother knew what it was like to live without the blessing and now that he saw it for what it really was, he was deeply grateful.

After Adam took all that God had given him and squandered it on a piece of fruit, he was the "lost" son who hid from his Father. God came looking for him and found him. When God found him, He sacrificed an animal as the very first blood sacrifice for sin. In doing this, God began the process of salvation. God made "coverings" for Adam and Eve, and for their sin, *"...I counsel thee to buy of me...white raiment, that thou mayest be clothed, and that the shame of thy nakedness do not appear;..." (Rev 3:18 KJV).* When God clothed Adam and Eve, they were no longer naked. Now their hell bent disposition was covered.

Always prepared

The story of salvation began in the Garden of Eden the moment that fruit was consumed, and it continues to this day.

The father from our story of the prodigal son had been preparing a calf even before he knew the whereabouts of his son. The calf was fattened, or prepared, for the son's arrival at the moment of it. God prepared a Lamb for us. That Lamb was already slain for the occasion of Adam's return.

When his son returned, the father from our story says, *"Bring in the finest robe..."* God makes Adam and Eve the "finest robes" as He clothes them with Christ. Next is a ring for their fingers and sandals for their feet. Rings denote power and sandals denote movement. God had a Lamb slain from the foundation, He sacrificed an animal to symbolize the sacrifice of His Lamb, He took the skin of the animal and covered His humans, He gave them back their authority through the curse placed upon the serpent, and then He said, "Go", *"Therefore the LORD God sent him forth from the garden of Eden, to till the ground from whence he was taken." (Gen 3:23 KJV).* Adam was a prodigal son. In this way, we are exactly like Adam.

Sin was a necessary evil.

Free to be Holy

"But we have this treasure in earthen vessels,
that the excellency of the power may be of God, and not of us."
2 Corinthians 4:7

The Passionate Protaganist

I like to watch decorating shows. The thing I love about them is how the decorators can come into a space that is ugly and in disrepair and turn it into something beautiful.

My husband and I bought our home over twenty years ago. Since then we have transformed a very humble house into a beautiful home -- both inside and out. Looking back, I am glad we didn't have the money to just go out and buy something that was already nice. There is a great deal of satisfaction in taking something bad and making it good.

What we must understand about God is that He is just like us. The reason He is just like us is because He made us in His image. It is not that God likes the things that we like; it is that *we* like the things that *He* likes. If I like taking something ruinous and turning it into something beautiful, it is because God likes to take something ruinous and turn it into something beautiful. Mankind was "ruined" and needed to be made beautiful.

The Greatest Warrior of all

God is a great Warrior; He loves to do battle, *"And all this assembly shall know that the LORD saveth not with sword and spear: for the battle is the LORD'S, and he will give you into our hands." (1 Sam 17:47 KJV)*. One must have an enemy if one is to need this Lord Who is planning to battle for him. Not only are Satan and his host our enemies, we have an enemy within which is in agreement with them. The Lord of Hosts is needed here.

God doesn't shrink away from the battle because God doesn't lose. God never loses, *"Thine, O LORD, is the greatness, and the power, and the glory,* **and the victory***, and the majesty: for all that is in the heaven and in the earth is thine; thine is the kingdom, O LORD, and thou art exalted as head above all." (1 Chr 29:11 KJV emphasis mine)*. All one must do to gain victory in this battle over death and sin is to get on God's side.

The psalmist asks, *"Who is this King of glory? The LORD strong and mighty, the LORD mighty in battle." (Psa 24:8 KJV)*. What does God say in the face of evil? "Bring it on…I ain't afraid."

God would never have put us in a compromising position unless He had the power and the will to deliver us from it. No one has to lose this thing; the battle is the Lord's. We lose the battle against sin because we are so busy running from it that we never effectively battle against it. We need to see this thing as the Lord's battle. Our role in this battle is to have faith in this Lord, *"Fight the good fight of faith."* We must trust our Lord of Hosts to wage this battle for us.

"A rilly big shew"

We all love a good movie - the sadness and longing, the joy and ecstasy. We enjoy watching heroes at work. It thrills us when good triumphs over evil. We like to see sacrifice for love, and courage in the face of danger. We enjoy watching hatred and apathy turn into tenderness and passion. It lifts our hearts when obscured truth finally comes out.

We take time off of living our own lives and pay money to momentarily live vicariously through the figures on the big screen. We are drawn to all of these things. Something inside of us hungers for this kind of life. If we, made in the image of God, enjoy these things, that proves that God enjoys these things.

Take away the deliverance, suspense, passion, restored relationships, forging of new relationships, the bad guy, the trial, the hero, and the victory from any movie and what you have left is the garden of Eden: *B - O - R - I - N - G*.

Where would come the thrill if there were no hard times? The Holy Spirit is called the Comforter, but how would we ever need comfort without discomfort? How will we enjoy that precious moment when Jesus wipes away our tears if there aren't any to wipe away? Without adversity, what possible reason could there be to encourage? Would the arms of our Father seem less strong if they were not protecting from a particular evil? Without sin, would we go on eternally, never beholding His beautiful eyes of mercy? Would we forever live without experiencing the elation of being lifted from a pit and made to lie down in green pastures?

How can we understand the glory of light, unless we have experienced the gloom of darkness? How can we comprehend the value of loyalty unless we have, at some point, been betrayed? How can we appreciate the relief of peace if we have not become disquieted through anxieties and fears? How can we appreciate a lovely day unless we have experienced an unlovely day?

You see, every good thing from God has a negative counterpart. We can't even comprehend the idea of good unless we have experienced bad. This is why, in the beginning, God did not take away the darkness, or evil, from earth; He only added His light. As darkness and light stood side by side, the plot thickened.

I have sat in the lap of God and cried like a baby. In these times, He pulls His arms more tightly around me and assures me that everything is going to be all right. I own those moments eternally and I am glad for it. It was sin that got me into God's lap and it was God's lap that got me out of sin.

How boring

It is true, God *could* have sat Adam down in the garden and said, "Adam, I love you so much that if your life was in danger, I would heroically rescue you. And, if you ever had an enemy, I would bravely avenge you. If you ever felt lonely, I would lovingly comfort you. If you ever experienced confusion, I would enlighten you. If you were ever backed up against a sea, I would valiantly part it for you. If you died, I would powerfully raise you. If you got sick, I would supernaturally heal you. If you ever killed a man, I would compassionately forgive you. As a matter of fact, even if you killed my One and only Son, I would forgive you, and in lovingkindness, make Him suffer the punishment in your place." I can almost feel God's frustration as His words fell on ignorant ears. Perfect little Adam couldn't even begin to relate to these things.

Adam would have probably responded to these proclamations by saying, "That is wonderful! You'd do that for me? Shucks, God, that's awesome."

And God would unenthusiastically respond, "Yes, I would do that for you and it really would be awesome." And that would be the end of it. How boring. What do we talk about tomorrow? Without sin there could be no demonstration of these beautiful acts.

A Passionate Protagonist

Read the Bible. What do you find? Passion. The Gospel of John says that Jesus was the Word and the Word became flesh and dwelled among us. Did the "Word" change in order to compensate for Adam's sin? No. Adam's sin allowed the "Word" to be written exactly the way it is written because God is His Word and we cannot change Who God is.

God is a Hero in that He triumphs over evil, sacrifices for love, and boldly tells us to have courage in the face of danger. With God, the Truth always comes out on top. The Gospel is called the greatest story ever told, and it was a *true* story. Nothing on the big screen can compare with the drama in which we have been invited to partake.

We, as children of God, have been offered a lead role in God's great production called "Life". It has it all: Love and hate, sickness and health, laughing and crying, giving and receiving, danger and safety, etc... This life will keep us on the edge of our seat, that is for sure, but the end of the story is fixed: We win. All we have to do is trust our God and our sin-ravaged life will be glorious beyond anything a sinless life would have to offer.

A demonstrative God

God is a very demonstrative God, *"But God **demonstrates** His own love toward us, in that while we were still sinners, Christ died for us." (Rom 5:8 NKJV).* God is the great protagonist in our life drama. God has fun with His love; He wants to be our Hero. God wants to fight for us, deliver us, sanctify us, heal us, and prosper us. God is love and He desires to lavish that love on us. The Bible shows us this picture over and over.

The very best example of this is found in the book of Exodus. Apparently, God was enjoying Himself in the deliverance of the children of Israel. Many heroic feats took place in their epic escape from Egypt, the land of bondage. Let's take a visit and watch this amazing God:

I won't even take the time to speak of the amazing acts that led up to the Red Sea, but it is an impressive list:

- Making leprosy come and go.
- Turning a staff into a snake that ate the other snake-staffs.
- Turning water into blood
- Covering the land with frogs
- Covering the land with lice
- Covering the land with flies
- Plague of boils
- Plague of hail
- Plague of darkness
- The slaughter of all the Egyptian firstborn sons

This last plague was *the last plague*; the Pharaoh finally let the people go. This is where we will pick up the story.

As the multitude left Egypt, the Spirit of the Lord led them via a detour to the edge of the Red Sea. The Egyptians had followed them. This is odd because while they were in Egypt, *"All the Egyptians urged the people of Israel to get out of the land as quickly as possible, for they thought, "We will all die!" The Israelites took with them their bread dough made without yeast. They wrapped their kneading bowls in their spare clothing and carried them on their shoulders. And the people of Israel did as Moses had instructed and asked the Egyptians for clothing and articles of silver and gold. The LORD caused the Egyptians to look favorably on the Israelites, and they gave the Israelites whatever they asked for. So, like a victorious army, they plundered the Egyptians!" (Ex 12:33-36 NLT)*.

The Egyptians had been so severely plagued by God that they practically carried the children of Israel out of their land on their shoulders. The Bible says that the Israelites *spoiled* the Egyptians. They loaded them with goods for the trip so they would have no excuse to return. The message was clear, "Get out and stay out."

So why did the Egyptians follow them if they were in such a hurry to get rid of them? Because God wanted, a really big show, *"And once again I will harden Pharaoh's heart, and he will chase after you. I have planned this so I will receive great glory at the expense of Pharaoh and his armies. After this, the Egyptians will know that I am the LORD!" (Ex 14:4 NLT)*. Twelve times the Bible says that God hardened Pharaoh's heart.

God purposely hardened Pharaoh's heart so that God would receive great glory at his expense. This is worded even more explicitly in Romans, *"For the scripture saith unto Pharaoh, Even for this same purpose have I raised thee up, **that I might show my power in thee, and that my name might be declared throughout all the earth**." (9:17 KJV emphasis mine)*.

God specifically raised up the Pharaoh to do evil so that God's *name* would be declared throughout all the earth. What name would that be? God: the Great Deliverer. God wanted the earth to know that there was a Deliverer and He was God. The same God, who rose up Pharaoh for the purpose of showing off His deliverance power, also bent mankind toward sin for the very same purpose. It is only when man looks solely to God as his Deliverer that God gets the glory and renown He so richly deserves.

An atmospheric Phenomenon

God doesn't do anything in small measure. As the children of Israel left Egypt, an angel of God went before them as a pillar of fire that guided them by night and a pillar of cloud that guided them by day. These were no small pillars; they reached to the sky.

On this first day of the Exodus, the pillar of cloud went before them and guided them to the Red Sea. It appeared that they could go no further. The Egyptians thought they had them cornered. But watch what God does in this pillar, *"Then the angel of God, who had been leading the people of Israel, moved to a position behind them, and the pillar of cloud also moved around behind them. The cloud settled between the Israelite and Egyptian camps. As night came, the pillar of cloud turned into a pillar of fire, lighting the Israelite camp. But the cloud became darkness to the Egyptians, and they couldn't find the Israelites." (Ex 14:19-20 NLT).*

The Egyptians could not have failed to notice this natural phenomenon. An enormous pillar of cloud had been guiding their enemies since they left Egypt. Now that they were backed against the sea, this "natural phenomenon" picked up and moved from the front of this six hundred thousand plus crowd of Israelites and resituated itself smack in front of the Egyptian army. Now *the Egyptians* were looking into this guiding pillar.

The Egyptians had to become even more apprehensive when night fell and this pillar of cloud became a pillar of fire. This fire shed light on the Israelites while it left the Egyptians in utter darkness. I cannot even imagine this marvel in the sky.

The Egyptians knew what this God could do--they had been the recipients of His wrath through one plague after another. One has to wonder what they were thinking on this dark night when six hundred thousand Israelites, standing at the base of a fire that reached to the sky, disappeared in front of their very eyes.

If looks could kill

Our grandiose God was not finished. In the early morning, while the pillar was still a pillar of fire, God showed His face, *"And it came to pass, that in the morning watch the LORD looked unto the host of the Egyptians through the pillar of fire and of the cloud, and troubled the **host** of the Egyptians," (Ex 14:24 KJV).*

That had to be a sight. Can you imagine seeing the face of God come at you through a dark, billowing pillar of fire? And I'm thinking it wasn't a pleasant face He showed them because it says that He *troubled* them.

Think about that: God gave the Egyptians a nasty look. And, it wasn't a fleeting look. Apparently, He stared at them for some time because it says that He did this through the pillar of fire *and* the pillar of cloud. He began His taunting in the early morning through the fire and then continued it through the cloud when the sun came up.

Drive like an Egyptian

Then, as the Egyptians pursued the children of Israel, God took it a step further, *"And took off their chariot wheels, that they drave them heavily:..." (Ex 14:25a).* God took the wheels right off the chariots that the Egyptians were driving! Come on. I like this God. I would not want to be an Egyptian in this battle.

We know what happens next, *"And Moses stretched out his hand*

Free to be Holy

over the sea; and the LORD caused the sea to go back by a strong east wind all that night, and made the sea dry land, and the waters were divided. And the children of Israel went into the midst of the sea upon the dry ground: and the waters were a wall unto them on their right hand, and on their left. And the Egyptians pursued, and went in after them to the midst of the sea, even all Pharaoh's horses, his (broken) chariots, and his horsemen." (Ex 14:21-23 KJV parenthesis mine).

God was keeping an eye on the Egyptians all night while Moses stretched out his hand over the sea. A strong east wind opened the sea and dried its bed. When this task was finished, God allowed the children of Israel to escape through the sea and also allowed the Egyptians to pursue after them to their death.

```
Easier yes, better?  No.
```

Now, don't you think there was a much easier way to guide the children of Israel? Of course there was. God could have constructed a bridge or equipped them with boats. God could have taken them by a different route; after all, they ended up walking for forty years anyway! Can you imagine the width of the gap in the sea that enabled the spilled waters to completely overcome the entire Egyptian army all at once? This was a very splashy event.

God likes splashy. Walls of water, probably hundreds of feet in the air, were on either side of them. Could they see fish; was it like a big aquarium? How crazy is it that they weren't walking in sludge up to their hips? God dried a soaking wet seabed! With a wind that fierce, I don't know how anyone was left standing. I can picture God with His big blow dryer, pin pointing that seabed. This is a big deal! God is a very dramatic God!

```
This is Who He is
```

What I want you to get from this picture is that God had all of this drama inside of Him before He made man. He still does. This is Who God is. This is how His love shines. Sin wasn't supposed to be some horrible thing that happened to humankind. Rather, sin was the vehicle by which God could be God. We must not let sin stand in the way of the very thing God used it to do -- draw us closer to Him by showing us His merciful and glorious power.

Underdogs

We like to play games because we like to win. Would we still enjoy the games without the possibility of losing? The best victories are indeed the ones that come from behind! This is the way we enjoy life. We love to see the underdog end up in a place of victory. God made the Israelites underdogs so that He could get the glory!

In the same way, God made us underdogs so that when our victory came it would be that much more glorious. Being made in the image of god, we are passionate beings that are not satisfied with spending our days in a Daisy patch. We like to get in there and mix it up. We are like God. We like the things God likes. God likes suspense and thrills therefore, we like suspense and thrills.

Let's say a group of children got together and formulated a football team. They practiced and became very good. What is the only way they can showcase their talent? Don't they need an opponent? We could watch them practice, but how does that provide us with an example of how good they are? Who is the winner when one beats himself? Many go to training camps to watch professional teams practice; many more go to the contests to see who is best.

And the children of Israel did evil...

I'd like to draw your attention to three interesting periods of rebellion and rest concerning the nation of Israel as is dictated in the book of Judges. We will use the New Living Translation of the

Bible and begin with the first incidence, which is found in the third chapter:

> *"**The Israelites did what was evil in the LORD'S sight.** They forgot about the LORD their God, and they worshiped the images of Baal and the Asherah poles. Then the LORD burned with anger against Israel, and he handed them over to King Cushan-rishathaim of Aram-naharaim. And the Israelites were subject to Cushan-rishathaim for eight years. But when Israel cried out to the LORD for help, the LORD raised up a man to rescue them. His name was Othniel, the son of Caleb's younger brother, Kenaz. The Spirit of the LORD came upon him, and he became Israel's judge. He went to war against King Cushan-rishathaim of Aram, and the LORD gave Othniel victory over him. **So there was peace in the land for forty years.** Then Othniel son of Kenaz died."*
> (Judg 3:7-11 NLT emphasis mine)

And so we have a story of sin, consequences, and deliverance. The children of Israel did evil in the sight of the Lord, God gave them over to a pagan ruler for eight years, they cried out, and finally God fills a man with His Spirit and uses him to deliver them. And then we have rest for forty years.

Immediately following the slight mention of four decades of sweet peace, we read the following:

> *"**Once again the Israelites did what was evil in the LORD'S sight**, so the LORD gave King Eglon of Moab control over Israel. Together with the Ammonites and Amalekites, Eglon attacked Israel and took possession of Jericho. And the Israelites were subject to Eglon of Moab for eighteen years. But when Israel cried out to the LORD for help, the LORD raised up a man to rescue them. His name was Ehud son of Gera, of the tribe of Benjamin, who was left-handed..."* (Judg 3:12-15 NLT)

Again we have a situation where the children of Israel did evil in the sight of the Lord, the Lord handed them over to a pagan king, (this time for eighteen years), they cried out, and finally God delivered them. The story continues as it details exactly how God used Ehud to deliver Israel and then culminates in these verses:

> "*So Moab was conquered by Israel that day,* **and the land was at peace for eighty years**." *(Judg 3:30 NLT)*

So here again we have a situation where we have a story of sin, consequences, and deliverance, followed by a very specific period of rest. This time the rest is not forty, but eighty years. Again, there is no story attached to the period of rest. Half a verse is dedicated to its mention and then we are done.

Can you guess what happens next? Just two verses later:

> "*After Ehud's death,* **the Israelites again did what was evil in the LORD'S sight**. *So the LORD handed them over to King Jabin of Hazor, a Canaanite king. The commander of his army was Sisera, who lived in Harosheth-haggoyim. Sisera, who had nine hundred iron chariots, ruthlessly oppressed the Israelites for twenty years. Then the Israelites cried out to the LORD for help.*" *(Judg 4:1-3 NLT)*.

So again, the children of Israel did evil, God put them under a pagan ruler, (this time for twenty years), and they cried out. The balance of this chapter tells the story of God's deliverance through His chosen vessels, going into some gory detail about how the captain of the host, Sisera, was murdered and mentions that before all was said and done, *"and all the host of Sisera fell upon the edge of the sword; and there was not a man left."*

The fifth chapter of Judges is comprised of Judge Deborah's song immortalizing God's many acts of deliverance of the children of Israel. When the song was completed, the chapter closes with these words:

"Then there was peace in the land for forty years."

And, just as with the other periods of peace, we have no mention of how these years went other than the fact that they experienced peace. And, as we have come to expect, in the very next verse we are met with the following:

"Again the Israelites did what was evil in the LORD'S sight. So the LORD handed them over to the Midianites for seven years." (Judg 6:1 NLT)

Three times the children of Israel did evil in the sight of the Lord, were handed over to pagan kings for a period of years, cried out to the Lord, and finally were delivered and given a forty, then an eighty, then another forty year rest before they immediately fell back into sin.

Who exactly was responsible for these periods of rest? Surely the children of Israel did not plot and scheme to be "good" for forty years, and then eighty years, and then forty years again. It is obvious that God orchestrated these rest periods. So, if God ordains and controls periods of rest, why wouldn't He just give everyone rest forever so that no one would rebel ever? If God is all about peace and rest, while He, evidently, is the only One Who can provide those things, then why would He lift that peace and rest at pre-determined times?

And, three times we watched the Bible give all the attention to the rebellion, the bondage, and the deliverance while it barely mentions the huge bulks of time where there was rest. Why was this rest period ignored as though it had no value for either praise or instruction? If God is all about everything going along smoothly, shouldn't He be focusing on that rest period equally as much as He focuses on the other?

From these stories, we can only conclude that, concerning our earthly existence, God is keenly interested in the battles and is only vaguely interested in the periods of peace. Evidently, there was purpose in every battle. He is the Lord of Hosts.

`Unbelievable!`

Although there are many such stories when it comes to the Chicago Bears, I would like to share what happened in one particular game. It is the year 2006 and the Chicago Bears are 5-0 on the season. They have come to Arizona to play the Cardinals. Arizona wasted no time in gaining an early lead. They were at the top of their game. The Cardinals were passing well, running well, and getting all the right blocks on offence while their defense was soundly shutting down the Bears.

On the other side of the field, the Bears were doing everything wrong. Chicago turned the ball over to Arizona *six* times. The Bears were missing passes, missing blocks, missing opportunities, and most notably, missing points. Early in the third quarter, the score was 20-0. It looked like there was no way the Bears were going to win. Being a long time fan, I found it difficult to watch.

`Don't count them out yet`

But then something unexpected happened. In the final seconds, the Chicago Bears won that game. It happened so fast and so nondescript that when the game was over, there was a momentary silence and an air of disbelief on the field, in the announcer's box, and in living rooms all across America. After allowing the Cardinals to deftly outplay them at every level of the game, somehow the Bears found a way to win that game.

Not only did Arizona end up with **double** the yardage on passing and rushing, and only two turnovers to the Bears' *six*, but the Cardinal's offense made *three* touchdowns while the Bears did not score even one offensive touchdown in the entire game. Blink, blink…did they really win?

Free to be Holy

After the game, one of the announcers said something like this, "Well, in football we are used to records being broken. But, to come from a 20-0 deficit in the third quarter and win without one single offensive touchdown has not happened in 100 years of football." And with that he tore up his card of stats and threw it in the air. What an exciting game.

You can still win

I felt sorry for the Arizona Cardinals. They left that field stunned. How did this happen? I wouldn't have wanted to be in that locker room. But, let's go to the Bear's locker room. Although I wasn't there, I think it is safe to assume there were many who were looking up to the heavens and praising God. A game like that could make a believer out of anyone.

I don't think a single player on the Chicago team would dare brag about that game. If there existed any praise, it would have to be directed toward God. That was one ugly performance and I don't think anyone thought that the Bears deserved that victory, nevertheless, a victory is what they had.

When the Bears defensive linebacker, Brian Urlacher was interviewed he said, "The coach gave us a hard time at half time, but he left us believing that we could still win that game and that is what we needed to hear."

Is there a message?

It wasn't until the following day that I began to wonder if God was showing me something through that game. This "game of life" that we are playing against the devil is never a pretty one. I can only speak for myself, but Satan has outrun me, out thrown me, blocked my passes, knocked me down, made me continuously cough up the ball, and invaded my territory way too many times.

Satan scored over and over while I blundered my way through this game not gaining a single offensive point. In the midst of the battle, God told me what I needed to hear, "You can still win." I went back to the game and the ugliness continued, but, blink, blink...the game is over and I win. I'm not even sure how it happened, but I won. I didn't deserve to win, but I won.

I heard a Christian once say, "My Dad's the Ump and we play till I win." I couldn't agree more. And it will be a magnificent game. The stories of that game will be told throughout eternity. The glorious moments will be immortalized. There is no bad news. If it looks bad at any point, it only means that the game isn't over yet. There is always hope. One of the things I look most forward to in eternity is hearing everyone's stories about God's victorious ways in their lives.

Glory to God

In the book of Judges, God commissioned Gideon to fight the Midianites. God had specific instructions concerning this war, *"The LORD said to Gideon, "You have too many warriors with you. If I let all of you fight the Midianites, the Israelites will boast to me that they saved themselves by their own strength." (Judg 7:2 NLT).*

Throughout the Bible, God sets up His people in such a way that it is impossible for them to win without Him. In this way, God keeps His children dependent on Him. As long as we are dependent on God, we will win and we will be able to enjoy the fruits of that dependent relationship along the way. That is exactly the way God planned it and that is exactly why He subjected us to vanity.

Bonding

Noted author and Christian speaker, Gary Smalley, recommended that families camp together. He went on to say that the more things went wrong on that camping trip, the better it would be for the family. Going through trials together causes humans to bond and get to know one another at deeper levels. If this is true of us, then it is true of God. If God wanted to bond with us, He needed to take us on a troublesome camping trip.

Were Adam and Eve bonded with God? I don't think so. I think that is why we see such a lack of passion in the garden before the first sin. Eve gave to Adam and he ate. It almost makes me want to cry.

Let's tell a story about a man named Bob who was married to a woman named Kim. Bob is very blessed because Kim is a perfect wife. One day an attractive stranger walks up to Bob and offers him sexual favors. Bob, without skipping a beat, says, "Sure!" and takes this woman to a hotel.

Does Bob love Kim? We can't prove it by his actions. *"And when the woman saw that the tree was good for food...she took of the fruit thereof, and did eat, and gave also unto her husband with her; and he did eat."* Did Adam and Eve love God? We can't prove it by their actions. Eve did no more than give in to a thirty-second discussion; Adam did nothing more than open his mouth for the fruit. The lack of fight in that garden convinces me that Adam and Eve did not even understand the concept of love.

What happens in movies as a result of misfortune? The characters introduced in the beginning end up having very different relationships in the end. Bonds are forged through calamity. This is just how it works. God wants to bond with us. Our Lord knows that if we get in there and mix it up with Him, we will draw closer to Him than if our lives were just simple walks in a garden.

We see the best come out of humans when they are in the midst of tragedy. We see heroic actions in war and in calamity. We saw it during and after the events that took place on 9/11. Man, made in the image of God, is most like God when adversity strikes. God, being like man, also shines brightest amidst the darkness of disaster. Bad brings out good in God, and the man whom He made in His image.

Gotham City

I like to think of God as Batman, the earth as Gotham City, and the devil as the Riddler. It seems a terrible metaphor, however, it is fitting. What made the comic strip *Batman* so unique is the fact that the superhero lived in, and saved people out of, a place called Gotham City.

Gotham City was a terribly evil place. It was dark, dank, and decrepit. The buildings were old and in disrepair. Windows were broken and entrances barred. Strangers lurked in dark alleys as debris blew across the cold, hard streets. A foul mist from the sewers rose through the manhole covers while nearby vultures pecked at dead rodents. The criminals, hidden from sight, planned their next caper.

Batman did not earn his notoriety by walking an old lady across a street in a place called Pleasantville. We are not drawn to stories of this nature. Gotham City was an evil city that was being held captive by criminals. Batman dove right into that evil and delivered its victims and *that* is what entertained us.

God knows this planet is polluted with demonic waste; all the better to showcase our great Hero and His marvelous acts. And, just as Batman's antagonists marveled at his prowess, so God's enemies do the same. Satan and his host of demons are relegated to give audience to God's amazing power against, and amidst their very own evil. God's Word is rich in decisive victories over Satan right in the heart of this "Gotham City".

Free to be Holy

What kid doesn't want a superhero for a Father? Well, we have one. When we find ourselves in trouble, with grandeur, God puts on His striking outfit, *"As the appearance of the bow that is in the cloud in the day of rain, so was the appearance of the brightness round about. This was the appearance of the likeness of the glory of the LORD."*, rides in on His cloud, and becomes whatever the situation demands as He delivers us from the hand of our enemy. God is my Hero.

God has all of this drama within Him and He simply cannot live it out without an enemy. There is no victorious battle when there are no enemies. How does good fight good? Do we really believe God would be satisfied without also being victorious?

> *"The Lord stands at your right hand to protect you. He will strike down many kings in the day of his anger. He will punish the nations and fill them with their dead; he will shatter heads over the whole earth. But he himself will be refreshed from brooks along the way. He will be victorious." (Psa 110:5-7 NLT)*

An away game

In sports, it is always a plus to have the home field advantage. However, God's power so outdistances and outdoes the power of the enemy that our Lord boldly triumphs over the devil right in his own backyard. God does not afford Himself any handicaps. He will beat Satan right in his rat-infested living room. There will be no offering of excuses or mistaking Who is truly powerful.

God gave Satan every advantage. He had his own planet and was given a strong military force. God even went as far as to bend His own creation toward evil to give Satan a running start. Through this subjection to vanity, Adam disobeyed God and gave the devil authority over man. This was all to show Satan that against all humanly odds, God could beat him with both hands and feet nailed to a cross. We cannot even begin to understand this magnificent

God. He is larger than life and He wants everyone to know it.

`Doesn't this seem wrong?`

Does it seem like God is a bit sadistic? At times it does, especially when we are in the midst of suffering. But how else would we really be able to experience this extraordinary God? After all, we only need stay in our suffering until we cry out for deliverance, not a moment longer. We can get into the grandeur of this thing whenever we would like.

God is just waiting for that day when we figure out that He is on our side. He longs for us to see the sufferings of this life for what they really are: Great victorious adventures that are intended to bond us so closely to Him that we become inseparable.

Look what happened to Nathan the moment he turned his eyes toward God. In the space of twenty-four hours his entire being was instantly and radically changed both inside and out. God is always on time and our battles always bear wonderful fruit.

`The valley speech`

Why was Nathan's deliverance so instantaneous? Nathan was in the valley. Through all of his trials he finally got to the bottom of the mountain of self. All of his efforts had ended him up in dire straights. Nathan came up close and personal to who he was without God and he didn't like what he saw. Though he has always been of a strong heart, he knew that he didn't own what it took to beat himself. He cried out in utter wretchedness thus, he received utter deliverance.

`Change is good`

My love and appreciation for God has grown by leaps and bounds as I have learned these amazing Truths. I used to walk around saying things like, "Why are You doing this to me? Why am I so bad? When is this going to end? Where are you? I am tired of praying this. Please talk to me." It was pathetic. I am sure I heard from God here and there, but I was so shaky about basic Truths that I was constantly being drawn away from Him. I was unskillful in the word of righteousness and my relationship with God showed it.

Since I have learned and applied these Biblical Truths I walk around saying things like, "Your Word, oh Lord, is a fire of power within me. I don't know what I would do without Your unfailing Word. You are an amazing God and I stand in awe of You. Your sweet presence makes me melt inside. I am so glad we understand each other and are free to love one another. I am so blessed by Your Presence and direction in my life. Thank You, Dad, I love You."

I talk to God all day long. I know it sounds a bit melodramatic but what you have to understand is that God *is* melodramatic. He loves a mushy love story. God didn't have to part the sea. He didn't have to stare through the cloud. He didn't have to change the Pharaoh's heart. He didn't have to come down on a mountain and make it quake and billow with dense smoke.

God chooses to act in a melodramatic way because He is a grand Being. He so far outdistances evil that it takes a huge production to even begin to do justice to it. God's intention was to act in such a magnificent manner that His name would be proclaimed throughout all the earth. Mission accomplished.

Sometimes there is no conversation between God and me. Sometimes we enjoy things together in silence. Other times we get into great theological discussions as we go back and forth across the pages of the Bible. There are even times when we laugh and kid each other. I cannot express how the truths found in *Free to be Holy* radically changed my relationship with God.

Nathan had heard this message his entire life. I began to live by faith while he was in the womb and I began to understand righteousness when he was six. When he came to the end of himself, he knew there was a God Who would meet him there.

God wanted us to have the best possible lives. The only way to do that was to inject the worst possible death. If the only way that I can experience God's greatness is through adversity, (and I cannot think of another), then so be it, *"Many are the afflictions of the righteous: but the LORD delivereth him out of them all." (Psa 34:19 KJV).* The Lord promises to deliver us out of all of our afflictions, not some of them…all of them. The Lord is not slack concerning any of His promises.

No pain, no gain

If you are in the middle of something horrible, don't worry; it is worth it. It may not seem like it right now, but God always comes through in the end and the end promises to be worth whatever we have to go through to get to it. Imagine how Nathan felt in those last moments before his deliverance. His worldly options were gone. His looked like a hopeless situation.

I know full well what it is like to feel forsaken, lost, and without hope. I have shed my share of tears. As a matter of fact, I think I have shed my share, and the share of several others. As the Psalmist said, *"I am weary with my groaning; all the night make I my bed to swim; I water my couch with my tears." (Psa 6:6 KJV).* I have been through things that I never dreamed possible. There were times that I thought that God hated me. Trust me when I tell you that I am akin to pain.

Jesus was proof that not only does God care about our pain and suffering, He was willing to suffer it Himself and be present with us through all of it. God shows Himself in deliverance, yes, but He also shows Himself in compassion, comfort, and patience while we are still a prisoner of our pit.

Not forsaken

We are not alone in this thing. Jesus warns against grieving the Holy Spirit because He is here shouldering this burden with us. The Holy Spirit is so involved in our lives that He is moved emotionally. Grief is an emotion. We have a true, living, touchable, powerful, amazing God Who cares for us so much that He wanted to walk through this by our side.

The twenty-third Psalm beautifully illustrates the inexpressible glory of having the God of Mercy by our side through this delivery process.

> *"The LORD is my shepherd; I shall not want.*
> *He maketh me to lie down in green pastures:*
> *he leadeth me beside the still waters.*
> *He restoreth my soul: he leadeth me in the paths of*
> *righteousness for his name's sake.*
> *Yea, though I walk through the valley of the shadow of*
> *death, I will fear no evil: for thou art with me;*
> *thy rod and thy staff they comfort me.*
> *Thou preparest a table before me in the presence of*
> *mine enemies: thou anointest my head with oil;*
> *my cup runneth over. Surely goodness and mercy shall*
> *follow me all the days of my life: and I will dwell*
> *in the house of the LORD for ever."*
> *(Psa 23 KJV).*

Looking for love in all the right places

God looks for us in the valleys, not on the mountain peaks. Thank You, God, the valleys are transitory; we do not have to live long in them. Nathan was delivered from his valley the moment he looked up. The valleys are not pleasant places, but thankfully, they are temporary places. And, I must add, necessary places.

We never saw Batman in a brightly lit café drinking a mocha smoothie. He didn't loiter near the checkout line and wait for someone who was thirty-two cents short so that he could blow in and save the day with his pocket change. No, it was into dark alleys and condemned buildings that he went. Batman was looking for those who were in grave danger.

So, if you are in a pit, look up! Your redemption draweth nigh. God is looking for you. When we have exhausted all human reasoning and resources, our God, with eyes that can penetrate the darkest night, will see us and swoop in to deliver us. As He does, we will fall in love with Him more deeply than we ever had before, and we will find ourselves pressing in closer to this loving and powerful God.

I was watching someone on television who found himself in a high state of anxiety. His friend asked him, "Are you a religious man?" He answered, "I am now." Adversity drops us to our knees so that God can lift us up. God gets the glory, while we get the blessing. Everyone wins. Who needs the movies now?

To whom little is forgiven

Although the pain I have suffered is beyond my description, I am left feeling sorry for those who have had it easy. They will never know God the way I do because they will never need Him the way I did, *"Wherefore I say unto thee, Her sins, which are many, are forgiven; for she loved much: but to whom little is forgiven, the same loveth little." (Luke 7:47 KJV).* I guess when it is all said and done I will be glad that I loved much.

In a family way

Earlier, when we considered the creation account, we saw that Jehovah Elohim breathed into Adam the moment he was formed just as a baby takes his first breath when he exits the womb.

What is the second thing a baby does? Cry. A baby is created in the womb, birthed into the earth, given breath, and then cries out because, suddenly his needs are not being met by the womb. The father and mother are there to comfort and bring deliverance. Now we have a family who will go through many ups and downs, all the while forging loving, everlasting relationships.

The human, adam, was created in the spiritual realm, birthed into the earth, and given the breath of life. This human went on to sin his way into a curse so that he would cry out. Father is there to comfort. All of humanity has followed this pattern. Now we have a family who will go through many ups and downs, all the while forging loving, everlasting relationships.

Cry out

My son didn't need a lot of theology and doctrine to find God; he needed to be desperate. Nathan needed to be slopping hogs and drooling over their meal. That is pretty close to the picture we got when we looked into his pit. Adam didn't need doctrine; he needed something awful to happen. Imagine what it was like for Adam and Eve to have their eyes opened for the first time to the Truth of their sinfulness. Good and evil stared them in the face and made them want to run and hide.

Adam and Eve did not sit around and discuss their newfound awareness, *"And the eyes of them both were opened, and they knew that they were naked; and they sewed fig leaves together, and made themselves aprons."* (Gen 3:7 KJV). All of this in one verse! Adam and Eve suddenly knew they were naked. That means that, immediately, deep shame flooded their beings. The Scriptures tell us that we need our garments of righteousness, *"So that the shame of thy nakedness not be seen."*

Prior to their sin, the closest Adam and Eve came to the knowledge of good and evil is in the law they were given to not eat of the fruit. Even this tiny bit of knowledge was enough to empower them to sin. Imagine what it was like to have all knowledge of good and evil poured upon them all at once. Adam and Eve's minds were filled with all thoughts of evil while their sin natures inclined them toward those thoughts. It is no wonder they ran and hid.

Adam and Eve wasted no time in trying to find a way to cover up. Our verse says that they sewed fig leaves together and made themselves aprons. They were not in the process of sewing; they had already made themselves aprons. But, because their bodily nakedness was only an earthly suit that symbolized their spiritual nakedness, their true problem remained unattended.

That is why when, *"...they heard the voice of the LORD God walking in the garden in the cool of the day... Adam and his wife hid themselves from the presence of the LORD God amongst the trees of the garden." (Gen 3:8 KJV)*. Even though they were "clothed", Adam and Eve hid from God.

`God help me`

Something inside of us hungers and thirsts for God and when that hunger is enticed to the surface through adversity, only God will do. It is our natural inclination to hide and it is our natural inclination to cry out to God. Even those who are unbelievers cry out to God in times of desperation. How many times have we answered the call of God from our hiding place?

We were made to cry out to God from the very depth of our being. Adam could only go as far up as he could go down. Adam didn't go down until he sinned, therefore, Adam could not go up until he sinned. Adam was on a nice, boring, even keel until he went down. And then the drama of deliverance began.

Contrast

Let's think about the idea of contrast for a moment. Using contrast is the best way to get a clear picture. If we are looking for the color white amidst several shades of gray that lead up to white, it may take us some time to find the true white. However, if we put true black against true white, the differentiation is clear.

If God had wanted to make His goodness stand out and be very apparent to us, then He needed to contrast it with something. When a fireman saves a kitten from a tree, he may get a "thank you" and an appreciative smile. However, if this same fireman risks his life by entering a burning building to rescue a child, he is heralded as a hero and given much praise, and rightfully so.

The glorious deliverance is in direct proportion to the gravity of the situation. I'm sure Adam probably appreciated God and thanked Him and smiled at His goodness before sin entered. Now that sin has entered, we are awe-struck by the powerful acts of God.

It's a simple concept; the more contrast is used, the more distinct the picture. A backdrop of evil was the best place for God to show us His goodness in the clearest possible fashion. Sin produced this evil background. The brutal ravages of sin provide the perfect environment for God to show us the many faceted, glorious God He really is. Through bondage to sin, we get to see God in all of His glory.

The Rose of Sharon

> *"I am the rose of Sharon, and the lily of the valleys.*
> *As the lily among thorns,*
> *so is my love among the daughters."*
> *(Song of Solomon)*

The entire Bible shows a picture of the artwork of God's majesty splashed across an evil backdrop, *"the lily among thorns."* This was His plan. If I have a beautiful white lily, I will not display it against a white wall. As a matter of fact, I will look for the darkest possible wall in my home. I want every detail of that lily to be appreciated. I want the whiteness of it to stand out. I don't want to lose any of its beauty by allowing my lily to blend into its environment.

We have the Rose of Sharon and the Lily of the valley as our Lord and our God. God is our Rose in the good times and our Lily in the bad. Roses thrive in sun; Lilies thrive in shade. Should not our God be displayed in *all* of His glory?

God is beautiful and majestic beyond words. Lilies are *of the valleys*. How dare I relegate our Lily of the Valley to a park bench on a sunny day? How would I then be able to distinguish His beauty from His beautiful environment? But, if I can only learn to appreciate the dark background of this evil world for what it is, I will be able to clearly see every facet of God's beauty.

When my white lily is displayed against a dark background, I notice and appreciate the lily. When God' goodness is displayed across the blackness of evil, I notice and appreciate my God.

Atom

Science is a wonderful teacher of Biblical principles. For our last example, we will look to this field for evidence of the beauty of the sin nature.

When God formed this world and set the seasons in motion, He made everything in such a way that it would scream of His existence. That is because, *"...the invisible things of him from the creation of the world are clearly seen, being understood by the things that are made..."* When we see a thing in the natural realm,

Free to be Holy

we are seeing a picture of a spiritual Truth. One cannot be an honest scientist long who ignores the existence of God. We are going to be scientists for a moment and look into the smallest, most foundational part of all matter: The atom.

Elementary

Everything in life is made up of basic elements and combinations thereof. For example, gold is a basic element and is made up of gold atoms, whereas hydrogen and oxygen atoms combine to form water molecules. The atom is the smallest part of any element, that is to say, an atom is the smallest portion into which an element can be divided and still retain its properties.

An atom is made up of a dense, positively charged nucleus inhabited by positively charged particles called *protons*, and neutrally charged particles called *neutrons*, and is surrounded by orbits of negatively charged electrons. Hence, the atom has positive, negative, and neutral aspects. Together they work to make up all matter in this natural realm.

The atomic model

The negative electrons, which are repelling each other and causing a great deal of movement through this repulsion, are held in orbit by the law of magnetism to the positively charged nucleus. When heat is added to the equation, the electrons must jump farther from the nucleus and then return to their original positions when they cool. As they return, they give off light energy; the wavelength of the light depends on how far the electrons jump. The hotter the heat, the further they stray, and the longer the light trail upon return.

If an atomic nucleus were as large as a period on this page, the atom would have a diameter equal to one-half of the length of a soccer field. So we see that the positive nucleus is much smaller than the electronic field surrounding it. However, this nucleus is so positively powerful that it can keep everything in orbit no matter how crazy it gets.

In an atom, it is obvious that the nucleus is winning the battle. The electrons are not traveling any further than the nucleus will allow. Even in the case where heat is applied and the electrons move further away from the center, they will begin to return the moment the heat stops. This drawing away is a temporary condition. The nucleus holds all power and control over the electrons in the atom.

```
The "adamic" model
```

Let's make Adam the atom, God the Proton, Jesus the Neutron, the negatively charged particles can be hell dust, and the light trail is God's glory of deliverance for all the earth to see.

God, the Proton, is such because He is positively energized and He keeps everything together. Jesus, the Neutron, is such because He is the Mediator between God and man. Hell dust, representing the electrons, is such because the hell dust is what causes us to be in a constant state of turmoil.

Jesus "neutralizes" the energy field between our negative hell dust factor and our positive God, which allows the two to function at a safe distance from one another. The light trail is such because the glory of the return is in exact proportion to the distance traveled, *"She who has been forgiven much loveth much."* The bigger the trial, the more glorious will be the deliverance.

Adam, the atom, is such because he is made up of a center containing God the Positive Power and Jesus the Neutralizer, and he has a negative energy field.

Jehovah Elohim first formed man of the dust of the earth then He breathed into him the breath of life. At that moment there were two forces taking place. We have both positive and negative charges active in Adam. Within Adam is the Power to hold all things together even while those things have the appearance of being crazy and out of control.

The good guys win

As well, in Adam, God the Proton and Jesus the Neutron are winning the battle. We were all made just like Adam. Jesus is keeping this whole thing neutralized by being the Mediator between God, the Positive, and our sin nature, the negative which allows God's positive force to keep us safely in our "orbit".

God uses His positive power to keep us at a safe distance. When the fiery furnace heats up, our sin nature will temporarily further us from God, just as Adam hid from God. As it cools down, we will return to God leaving a stream of light behind us such as was the case in the prodigal son.

Why wouldn't God use the most elementary particles of matter as a model to show us how man was formed and how he relates to his God and his environment? *"For the invisible things of him from the creation of the world are clearly seen, being understood by the things that are made, even his eternal power and Godhead..."* (Rom 1:20 KJV). The invisible "image of God, hell dust factor" concepts from the very creation of the world are clearly seen being understood by things that are made in this natural realm. We understand Adam by studying the properties of the very things that were used to make up Adam: Atoms.

In summary

We have uncovered a great many new concepts. Let's review them:

1. There are two realms of existence: The spiritual and the

natural.
2. Elohim created in the spiritual and Jehovah Elohim birthed these creations into the natural.
3. Nothing can exist in the natural unless it has first existed in the spiritual realm.
4. God subjected all of mankind to vanity so that He could deliver them from the bondage of corruption into the glorious liberty of the sons of God.
5. Adam was subjected to this very vanity when he was formed of the dust of the earth.
6. Adam was placed in a garden.
7. It was Adam's built-in vanity, or sin nature, which compelled him to eat of the fruit and die.
8. Because God is a Sower, He planted His dead seed so that He could raise His first Child, Jesus, through the bloodline of humanity, and then subsequently, raise us up in Christ.
9. At the time when Adam and Eve ate the fruit, they recognized that they were naked and needed to be covered.
10. God covered Adam and Eve's sin through the animal that was sacrificed for their clothing. This act was symbolic of a spiritual Truth that would not manifest for thousands of years: The crucifixion of the Lamb.
11. God then ushered in the curse over the serpent that told of his demise, and then over the man and the woman, which would produce the "bondage of corruption".
12. Having defeated the enemy, now through this very bondage of corruption God would show Himself strong in the deliverance of man.
13. This magnificent deliverance is used to draw man toward God through faith and proclaim God's name over all the earth so that others could learn to live by faith.
14. God's names are Who He is, not merely what He does, therefore, God had every intention of using all of the facets of Who He is to minister to mankind.
15. The examples that Jesus taught us through the shepherd who lost a sheep, the woman who lost a coin, and the prodigal son,

teach us that it is better to fail and be restored than to never fail at all.
16. God is very passionate and He draws us into a passionate relationship.
17. Passionate relationships are forged through adversity and deliverance.
18. Evil contrast is necessary for clear comprehension of good.
19. The things of God are clearly understood by things that are made; the atom is a model of Adam.
20. Sin was a necessary evil.

More than meets the eye

A Christian must understand that once he has been born into the spiritual realm, he is in the middle of an amazing tapestry of good and evil existing in both the natural and the spiritual realms. God separated the light from the darkness so that they would co-exist in the earth. Rather than seeing the darkness as a "problem", we must see it as the very vehicle that God uses to show us His glory and bring us into deep intimacy with Him.

In this strange existence of good and evil, we have the God of the universe on our side Who loves us and has provided all that is necessary to win every battle. When one pays attention to the happenings in the spiritual realm as much as the happenings in the natural realm, he begins to see things from God's perspective. There is much more to this life than what meets the eye.

Ruined...but wait

On the final night of a weeklong seminar, the teacher used pastels to create a gorgeous landscape picture. All the colors were bright and brilliant. At the moment we thought he was finished, our teacher "ruined" his picture by taking a piece of black chalk and haphazardly slashing lines through it. We were aghast as horrible black streaks now marred our once beautiful scene.

However, our wise teacher was not finished. He began to add foliage and flowers to the black lines that we now recognized as tree trunks. Contrasting plant life suddenly enhanced our picturesque landscape. The blackness of the branches made the beautiful background landscape stand out as though it were alive. The foliage and flowers on the trees were distinct against the light background and the dark trees. The picture ended up more striking after it had been "ruined" than before.

Sin did not really ruin anything. Sin added an element that enhanced the goodness of God. Yes, sin will be defeated, but not by the power nor by the will of man. Sin will be defeated as we exercise our free will to rest in God's way of doing things and trust Him to honor His Word and deliver us from it. God designed things this way and He has provided a Way to make it all even more beautiful in the end.

`Control tower, do you read me?`

We do have a God Who is in complete control and at rest on His heavenly throne. And because He is Three in One, we also have a God Who is here with us, helping us to birth all spiritual blessings in the heavenly places into the natural realm just as Jehovah Elohim birthed the spiritual creations of Elohim into the natural. We can rest in this God.

Laying his eyes upon Jesus, John the Baptist said, *"Behold, the Lamb of God Who taketh away the sin of the world."* In the spiritual realm, sin is taken out of the world. That means that, spiritually speaking, Christians are already holy just as God is holy in the same way that Jesus was slain spiritually before He was slain naturally. The cross worked backwards as well as forward because once a thing is done in the spiritual realm, it is as real as it will ever be. The Holy Spirit is here with us to help us birth our spiritually "real" holiness into the natural realm.

Free to be Holy

All sin that was ever committed and that would ever be committed was laid upon that sacrificial Lamb Who was nailed to a cross. God loosed His wrath to destroy them both. Abraham's willingness to kill Isaac was a natural realm picture of God's willingness to kill His Son. And just as Abraham was willing, because he knew that God could raise Isaac from the dead, so God was willing to sacrifice His Son because He knew He *would* raise Jesus from the dead.

God killed two that day two thousand years ago: Jesus and sin. Only One was raised, *"O death, where is thy sting? O grave, where is thy victory?"* There are many so-called "gods"; only One left behind an empty grave.

"Not by strength, nor by power, but by My Spirit saith the Lord."

The transformation from the bondage of sin into the blessing of holiness comes in the form of a promise, *"Whereby are given unto us exceeding great and precious promises: that **by these** ye might be **partakers of the divine nature**, having escaped the corruption that is in the world through lust." (2 Pet 1:4 KJV emphasis mine).* We escape the corruption that is in the world through lust and are made partakers of the divine nature through exceeding great and precious *promises*.

God put us in this mess and He has all the power, provision, and intention to deliver us from it, *"For the creature was made subject to vanity, not willingly, but by reason of him who hath subjected the same in hope, Because **the creature itself also shall be delivered from the bondage of corruption** into the glorious liberty of the children of God."*

It is time to relax and enjoy God in all of His glory and let Him show us how much He loves us. Christians are not looking for ways to get away with sin. God will deliver those who are crying out for a deliverer just as He delivered the apostle Paul, my son Nathan, and myself when we cried out. The person who is looking for a way to get away with sin does not even know God. The Spirit that has been birthed into the born again Christian cries out, "Abba Father." The Father will answer the cry of His beloved children.

"But we have this treasure in earthen vessels, that the excellency of the power may be of God, and not of men"

The reason we have this treasure of God in these frail, hell dust vessels is so that the supremacy of the power may be of God and not of men. This verse says it all. God does not expect a single thing from mankind so long mankind expects everything from God.

This sort of complete reliance upon God does not come naturally to us. This is just as it should be. God planned to use His deliverance process to prove to us that He is a loving and merciful God Who can be trusted. The more we see God work, the easier it will be to have faith in Him.

It is like a birthing process. Babies are birthed, or delivered into the world after a time of labor. The Bible tells us that we must labor to enter into the Sabbath rest of God, *"There remaineth therefore a rest to the people of God. For he that is entered into his rest,* **he also hath ceased from his own works***, as God did from his. Let us labour therefore to enter into that rest, lest any man fall after the same example of unbelief." (Heb 4:9-11).*

One time when I encouraged one of my sons to put something into God's hands, he responded to me by saying, "I hate it when people say stuff like that. I don't know how to put this in God's hands. Show me how." It's true; sometimes we do not really know how to enter God's rest. There are many "Christianisms" that are so ethereal that it is difficult to understand how to put them into practice. This is something we need to be taught.

The subsequent books in the *Free to be Holy* series go a long way to teach ethereal Christian concepts in a practical and understandable way. We will learn how to rest in God, how to battle effectively against sin, how to "give it to God", how to put *real* works with our faith, and how to trust Him for all things that are necessary for life and godliness. We will learn how to cease from our own works, join God in His throne room, get the necessary provisions for all of life and godliness, and enter into His rest.

Confusion will give way to a comprehension that will alter your life permanently.